OLD SKYE TALES

OLD SKYE TALES

Traditions, Reflections and Memories

with a selection from

Skye: Iochdar–Trotternish and Disctrict

William Mackenzie

edited by
Alasdair Maclean

Birlinn

This edition published in 2002 by
Birlinn Limited
West Newington House
10 Newington Road
Edinburgh
EH9 1QS

www.birlinn.co.uk

First edition
Skye: Iochdar – Trotternish and District 1930
and
Old Skye Tales 1934
Second edition
Old Skye Tales
MacLean Press, Skye, 1995

ISBN 1 84158 201 8

British Library Cataloguing-in-Publication Data
A catalogue record for this book is available
from the British Library

Typeset by eidetic, Edinburgh
Printed and bound by Cox & Wyman Ltd, Reading

Contents

William Mackenzie (1851–1935)

William Mackenzie was born in 1851 in Melness in Sutherlandshire, the son of Peter Mackenzie, who was born in Caithness, and Ann Mackay.

He came to Skye at an early age and attended school in Kensaleyre, where his father was schoolmaster. He also trained to be a schoolteacher and took up his first teaching appointment in Uig in 1870. Shortly after that, he married Janet Lamont from Keistal, with issue of three daughters and one son. In about 1879 he was appointed headmaster of Valtos School in Staffin.

The crofter agitation for better conditions of rent and tenure began about 1880 and Mr Mackenzie was active on behalf of the crofters at the sitting of the Napier Commission in 1884.

He retired from teaching in 1915 and was succeeded in Valtos by his eldest daughter, Abby, but continued to visit the school to teach the older boys navigation and to deputise for his daughter when she was necessarily absent from her duties.

He was a tall man of spare build, and, even in old age, maintained an erect bearing. He enjoyed working with wood until the end of his life and had an extensive knowledge of the types and qualities of various timbers. Like his father before him, he was also a keen angler.

In his retirement he began to write his reminiscences, which were published at intervals in the *Oban Times* newspaper from 1929. In 1930 these articles were brought together in book form as *Skye: Iochdar – Trotternish and District*. Further articles were combined in the book *Old Skye Tales* in 1934.

Mackenzie died in 1935, having been pre-deceased by his wife and all his family, with the exception of his eldest daughter. He is buried in an unmarked grave in the new cemetery at Skeabost.

Preface to Skye: Iochdar – Trotternish and District

To my fellow Skyemen, at home and abroad, I dedicate these few pages, and especially to my friends of Trotternish, among whom I spent my happy irresponsible boyhood, and whose sympathy in the sorrows of later years I valued and treasured. Many of the youthful companions of those far-away times are exiles in distant lands, and many, alas, have passed the bourne whence there is no return. To those exiled from the old homes, these pages may, perchance, enable them in fancy to tread again the hills and glens they trod in vigorous youth, *mu'n do chuir iad cul ri Eilean a' Cheo* (before they turned their backs on the Isle of the Mist), perchance awaken within them some tender feeling for the land they and I love – a love that will cease not till the night clouds hover, and the darkening shadows deepen. Perchance they may be a magnet attracting irresistibly the exile across seas and lands to visit in person the surroundings of the old home, renew the old friendships, and feast upon the old familiar landscapes, recalling the weird tales attributed to haunted mountain, glen, and corrie, visiting the fairy knolls, and dark lochs harbouring their monsters, treading a land storied with the ghostly past.

Begun in days of enforced idleness, memory recalled the old, and pictured afresh the new. Should these pages afford a meed of pleasure to those for whom they were written, and to others of the race, the writer will be amply rewarded.

An caill mi cuimhn' air comunn blath,
Na h-òigridh chàrdeil ghrinn,
Bhiodh leam ag cluich air feadh nam blàr,
'S a' manran mu na tuim.

Will I lose the memory of warm comradeship,
Of the comely friendly youths
Who were with me playing among the fields,
And dallying about the knolls?

William Mackenzie, 1930

Preface to Old Skye Tales

Responding to requests from many friends, far and near, for further tales of the romance, the glamour, the old beliefs, and the haunting wraiths of Eilean a' Cheo, I have penned the following pages, which I again dedicate to my fellow Skyemen, and Gaels in general. No-one is more sensible of its defects than the writer. For these defects, incidental to the author's eighty-fourth year, I crave the kindly indulgence of my readers. I take this opportunity of expressing my gratitude for the widespread support and appreciation vouchsafed to *Skye: Iochdar – Trotternish and District*. I trust a similar measure of support awaits this effort on behalf of our island homes. That support came from our great cities, equally with our rural homelands, and from every corner of our far-flung Empire, where Gaels carved out homes for the virile race from which they are sprung. In the silent hours of solitude, in the unconscious slumbers of the night, we may imagine their souls being wafted again to the hills and dales, to the glens and clachans which they or their forbears left with hearts bursting with dull sorrow, as they took a long, last farewell look on the hamlets of their youth. And we may imagine an experience, a mystical akinness to these silent shadowy beings, as they hover over the graveyard in the hollow, where sleep for centuries the loved ones gone before, whom they, in the fullness of their simple faith, believe will meet them on the further shore, where life's troubles cease, and parting is no more.

William Mackenzie,
Blarcrian, Culnacnoc, Portree

Note: For some family history supplied, the author acknowledges his indebtedness to Lt-Col. Martin Martin of Ostaig in Sleat, and Captain Nicol Martin of Glendale, the respective heads of the Martins of Beallach and Marishadder; to Major Norman MacLeod, Col. K.L. MacDonald DSO; also to the Rev. D.A. MacDonald DD, Kilmuir, whose encouragement was a leading factor in my 'Memories' taking this form.

WANDERINGS IN TROTTERNISH

Brae Trotternish lies between Portree and Sligachan lochs. Iochdar or Lower Trotternish is the north-east wing of Skye.

1 PORTREE

Port an Righ (Portree) is where James V landed on his mission to quell his turbulent island subjects, the capital of Skye. It is situated at the head of a land-locked bay, overlooked by an amphitheatre of houses. It is the gateway to a land teeming with tradition, romance, and weird tales of the dim and distant ages, wrapt in mystery, the attraction of people from every clime. Its memories warm the heart of the exiled native, kindling in his soul the bygone times and places of youth, inflaming in his heart the desire to again live over the old scenes, the magnet which, with tender feelings, draws him homeward again – homeward again, saying, 'Tha mi dol dachadh.' ('I am going home.')

Portree's communication is supplied by daily and weekly boats. The writer's early remembrance of this service seventy years ago was that carried on by Mr David Hutchison, to whom lies the credit of opening up the Western Highlands and Islands. The boats were the *Inveraray Castle* and *Mary Jane*. The latter still continues her career under the altered name of *Glencoe*. The early captains of the Hutchison boats plying into Portree were Sinclair and Beaton. The latter was a genial, affable gentleman, always solicitous for the comfort of his passengers. The former should have been in the army. At that time, the boats were anchored in the bay till the flowing tide permitted them to get alongside the old stone pier. Even today this pier would not be the worse of some more protection than it has. Mr Peter Macdonald was the steamer agent. He occupied the block of buildings later used as a bookseller and newsagent's shop. A peculiarity of his shop sign was that it was painted in script instead of the usual block letters. He died in 1873.

The old post office was a modest compartment in a shoemaker's shop and the shoemaker was also the postmaster. The police force consisted of an inspector and constable in Portree, a constable in Dunvegan and one in Strath or Sleat. The inspector was a MacKay from Lochaber and, though over sixty years of age, was a fine singer of the old clan and foray songs, now long forgotten.

The village contains three commodious hotels, which seasonally are quite inadequate to accommodate the ever increasing rush of visitors attracted by the beauties of the Misty Isle, and the mystic lure of Eilean a' Cheo is a magnet drawing such crowds that hotel accommodation must be booked far in advance. The oldest hotel is the Royal. The small thatched building to which Prince Charlie and his attendants repaired would be sadly out of place today. The earliest tenant whom the writer remembers is Mr John Ross, a *rosach mor*. The old Caledonian was a modest building, fronting the square, tenanted by Mr Lachlan Ross, later of the Royal Hotel, Stornoway, and, still later, the Royal Hotel, Portree. Mr Murchison succeeded in the Caledonian and the business was carried on by the family in more central premises. A hazy recollection of the Portree Hotel is the blackened ruin from which the present hotel emerged. Mr Simpson and Mr Robertson improved the Royal and Portree hotels respectively, so much that the hotels are equal to the best in the land, and the Caledonian is following suit. There are the usual plethora of churches. To the east of Portree is Creag nam Mor Shluagh (Rock of the Big Crowd). It is here the army of James V landed, and marched to, and encamped on, what is now known as the Square. The king himself, with his suite, landed at the river falling into the bay, and joined his army on the plain above. This imposing force must have made a deep impression on the recalcitrant chiefs and headmen who hurried to make their submission.

The names Bosville Terrace, Beaumont Crescent and Wentworth Street are reminiscent of an amazing romance in the life history of the seventeenth MacDonald chief, Sir Alexander. Sir Alexander MacDonald, 9th baronet, and 17th chief of the MacDonalds of Sleat, was married to Elizabeth Diana, daughter of a Yorkshire squire, Godfrey Bosville, who could show a pedigree almost as long as the MacDonalds'. A son, Godfrey, was born on 14 October 1775. He was the third child, and the second son. His elder brother, Alexander Wentworth, on the death of his father, succeeded to the titles and estates as 2nd lord MacDonald, and 18th chief of the MacDonalds of Sleat.

After his education at Harrow and Oxford, Godfrey, like his forbears, became a soldier. His father had recruited two regiments. One of these, the 76th MacDonald Highlanders, was disbanded at the close of the war. Godfrey's active services were many and varied, including the Continent, South Africa, West Indies and other spheres. The year 1797 was an eventful one in the life of the young soldier. It is recorded that when riding in the vicinity of Hampton Court, he espied in a villa garden a lovely girl. He was smitten by her charm, and somehow procured an introduction to the family. The reputed parents were Mr and Mrs Farley Edsir, tenants of a dairy farm. Godfrey proposed marriage. To his astonishment, he was told that his suit could not be entertained, as the young lady was expected to make a great match. He told Mr Edsir that a MacDonald of the Isles was a good enough match for anyone, beyond the status of the Edsirs. Thereupon Mr Edsir told him that the young Louisa Maria was not his child, but the daughter of HRH the duke of Gloucester, brother of George III, who had married secretly the Lady Almeria Carpenter, daughter of the earl of Tyrconnel. As the duke and duchess resided abroad, few knew about the marriage. This fact altered the complexion of the affair. The girl was named after her father's sister. Louisa was born on 6 January 1782, at Esher, Surrey, near Hampton Court, of which the duke was ranger, and the child was given to Mr Edsir, who was steward to the duke, to be brought up. Lady Almeria was given rooms in Holyrood Palace in 1809 and died there at the age of 57.

Louisa was sent back to school to Esher, and Godfrey returned to his military duties in Ireland. Before long, the impetuous and infatuated lover carried her off from school, taking her as his wife to Ireland, where he was on military duty. Being a Scotsman he married her there by 'mutual consent', according to the law of Scotland. The English and Irish laws do not recognise this form of marriage, and hence the troubles which followed. Godfrey still desired to have a church marriage in Ireland, but Louisa, fully believing that she and Godfrey were already man and wife, objected that Ireland was an out-of-the-way place in which to be married, and that when she had a church marriage, it should be a grand affair in England, when they got back there. But his duties in Ireland protracted his stay there.

The issue of the marriage were Alexander William Robert, born 12 September 1800; William, who died young, born on 29 August 1801; Louisa on 16 September 1802. She became countess of Hopetoun, wife of the 5th earl. Godfrey was constantly on service, not long in any place.

He was now Colonel MacDonald.

The church marriage took place on 29 December 1803. The issue prior to the church marriage at Norwich, according to the English law, would be illegitimate, provided that Colonel MacDonald's domicile was outwith of Scotland. Elizabeth-Diana was born 27 February 1804 (Elizabeth after Lady Elizabeth Carpenter and Diana after Lady MacDonald). She became Mrs Davidson of Tulloch. Julia, born 30 October 1805, became Mrs Charles Hudson. Susan Hussey, born 25 August 1807, became Mrs Richard Beaumont (Susan after Lady Susan Carpenter, marchioness of Waterford, Hussey after the countess of Tyrconnel). Godfrey William Wentworth, born 16 March 1809, was the first son, born after the Norwich marriage, and was afterwards the 4th lord MacDonald; James William was born 31 October 1810. Diana, born 12 April 1812, was afterwards Mrs Smyth of Heath (Diana after her aunt, Lady Sinclair of Ulbster, Diana MacDonald).

Before the birth of Godfrey above noted, his father and mother journeyed to Scotland, and on the 26th day of October, 1807, solemnly declared before Provost Forrest, Annan, that they had been engaged and betrothed to each other in Christmas week 1790, and from that period had understood themselves to be married. This Annan Declaration was signed by G. MacDonald, Lt-Col. 24th Regiment, Louisa Maria MacDonald, Richard Forrest, Provost, and Richard Graham and James Little, witnesses.

In 1805, after the death of William, duke of Gloucester, Mrs Edsir wrote a short statement that Louisa was not her child, embodying the facts above recorded, a true statement of the birth and parentage of Louisa. Papers in possession of Lady Almeria, which might have elucidated some points in this connection, were, at her request, buried with her.

After the elopement of Godfrey and Louisa, there is no evidence that her great-parents took the slightest notice of her. Her husband's relations, on the other hand, took the liveliest interest in the young couple. Col. William Bosville, the maternal uncle of Godfrey, Alexander, the 2nd lord MacDonald, and James, the other soldier of the family, were all kindly disposed.

In December, 1813, Colonel Bosville died, and left his Yorkshire estates to Godfrey in liferent, and specified that should Alexander Robert MacDonald, or any issue, become entitled to the MacDonalds' estates, the Yorkshire estates would go to Godfrey's heirs, according to their successive and respective seniorities. Col. Godfrey then assumed the name of Bosville and went to live at Thorpe Hall. He retired from the army in 1814 with the rank of General, and was known as General Bosville till 1824. In 1812 he was again on active service in the Peninsular War, with the result that he was appointed major-general. Lord MacDonald (his father) was one of the guardians appointed by Godfrey with the care of his family during his absence. It was Lord MacDonald who paid the Harrow bills of the eldest son, Alexander William Robert.

Several more children had by this time been added to the family group – Jane Bosville, born on 25 May 1815, unmarried; Marianne, born 27 July 1816, became Mrs Henry Turner; William was born at Thorpe on 20 September 1817; Octavia Sophia was born at Thorpe on 6 February 1819. She was afterwards Mrs Hope Johnstone.

Portree

In 1824 Alexander Wentworth, 2nd lord MacDonald and 10th baronet, Godfrey's elder brother, died unmarried, and Godfrey became 3rd lord MacDonald and 11th baronet and succeeded to the family estates in Skye, with Armadale Castle, built by his brother, as a residence. He now resumed the name of Macdonald after Bosville. Godfrey was proud of his Highland blood and famous descent, maintaining the old claims of the house of Sleat, of which he was the 18th chief and representative of the last Lord of the Isles. Glengarry did not approve of this, but though he formally objected, he did not take legal steps to enforce his claim. He, however, made himself so obnoxious that Godfrey challenged him to a duel. This did not come off. Glengarry urged Godfrey's brother, the 2nd lord, to acknowledge him, Glengarry, as the chief of the clan. Lord MacDonald wrote in reply, 'Dear Sir, till you prove that you are my chieftain, I am yours, MacDonald.' Godfrey's eldest son, Alexander, after his education, married Matilda Moffat Bayard, and they lived as the Hon. Mr and Mrs MacDonald.

Passengers aboard the steamer

In 1832 Godfrey died suddenly in Bridlington from a heart attack, aged 57 years; his widow survived him only two years, leaving a sad tragedy for his eldest son. Though the marriage by 'mutual consent' was a true marriage, it could not be recognised by English law. Be it said that Godfrey did all he could by re-marrying at Norwich, and by the Annan Declaration. It seemed quite clear to the parties concerned, but an eminent Scots lawyer declared the domicile at the time of marriage was English. The position for Alexander was not an enviable one, when he got the first hint that he was not Lord MacDonald. In spite of his father's will that he, the eldest son, should have the Scots honours and estates, and the second son, Godfrey William, should have the Yorkshire estates, the position was reversed. It was Godfrey who became 4th lord MacDonald by law of succession, and his brother Alexander became invested in the Thorpe estates, dropping the MacDonald name. Alexander set out in improving the estate of Thorpe. He declined to say or do anything in the difficult position. Lord MacDonald exhausted the revenues of his Highland estates and desired to sell a part of Skye. But as the estates were entailed, he could not. Finally, a private Act of Parliament was passed settling the Thorpe estates on Alexander Bosville, and the Scots estates on Godfrey, 4th lord MacDonald, with authority to sell some to satisfy his creditors.

In 1847 Alexander died, leaving two children, a son, Godfrey Wentworth Bosville, born in 1826, and a daughter, Julia, wife of the 8th lord Middleton. Godfrey succeeded his father at Thorpe. He married in 1841 Harriet, sister of the 8th lord Middleton. A son was born on 26 September 1865, but a fortnight later the father died, so that Godfrey never raised the question of descent. The son left was named Alexander Wentworth MacDonald, and was known, like his father, as Bosville. In 1886 he married Alice Edith Middleton. On 25 September 1887, Godfrey Middleton was born, and on 28 January 1889, a daughter, Celia Violet. Advised and pressed by Clanranald, he consulted Scots lawyers. Their advice was favourable to his claim. After some delay, the case was raised in May 1909. Lord MacDonald's trustees opposed the suit. The decision was adverse, and they appealed. This was again in Mr Bosville's favour. The case was then proceeded with, and after a time opposition was withdrawn. Lord Skerrington, after proof, pronounced in favour of Mr Bosville. The domicile was Scottish from birth. The soldier did not lose his domicile. Thus were the loves of Godfrey and Louisa vindicated. Alexander was given his place as 12th baronet and 19th chief. The writer often heard this old story spoken about in his youth. Alexander Wentworth MacDonald Bosville became Sir Alexander Bosville MacDonald of the Isles, 21st chief of Sleat and 14th baronet of Nova Scotia. After his claim was vindicated in the Court of Session, Sir Alexander took for a time residence at Duntulm, in sight of the ruins of the old castle occupied by the chiefs of the MacDonalds for untold centuries. From the foregoing pages it will be seen that the MacDonalds are connected with many of the highest families in the land. On more than one occasion they married into royalty.

Lt-Col. Valentine Vyvian Harvey DSO, who died in 1930, aged 44 years, was a direct descendant of Davidson of Tulloch, and Diana, daughter of the 3rd lord MacDonald mentioned in the foregoing.

The old tale of the writer's early days was that Godfrey married a dairymaid at Gretna.

There are three roads branching from the village, north, south and east. We follow the latter. On the right is Creag 'Ic Neacail, called after some Nicolson of Scorrybreac, also the Beall on the right. In the seaward face of the Beall is the Robber's Cave. It is about 300 feet from the bottom and 30 feet from the top. Here the pirate robber, Mac a' Choiteir, was afforded a wide vision, and could at the opportune moment intercept his prey, and secure a part of the contents of the small craft then plying. Forty years ago a rabbit trapper noticed several coins thrown out by a rabbit. Returning with a spade, he unearthed a treasure hoard of 200 pieces, all of ancient coinage, which is today in the Edinburgh Museum. What is likely is that Mac a' Choiteir, being hard pressed, hid his ill-gotten wealth and did not survive to reclaim it.

On the Bil or Beall near Portree there are the ruins of a church, and an old graveyard long forsaken. It possibly might have been the burial place of the Nicolsons centuries ago. There is an old saying in connection with the Nicolsons: 'Clann Mhicneacail a'Bhrochan, bithidh an t-uisge ann air latha am posaidh.' ('Nicolsons of the porridge: there will be rain on their marriage day.') Opposite Beal at Camus Ban (White Bay) there is a coal mine, abandoned, however, as being uneconomic. The improved methods of today might change this, and it might be yet a boon.

2 DR ALASDAIR BAN MACLEOD

An Dotair Ban (The Fair-Haired Doctor)

Tha mi 'n duil gu'm faigh sinn bàrd,
A ni dhasan rogha dàin,
Theid a sgriobhadh air a chàrn,
A nis o'n dh'fhàg a chainnt e.
　　　Mairi Higheann Iain Bhain

I hope we shall find a Bard
Who will compose a choice song for him,
That will be written on his cairn,
Now that he is without speech.
　　　Mary MacPherson

No more remarkable man than the Doctor Ban MacLeod appeared in our Western Isles for more than a century. As a surgeon, engineer, reclaimer of waste land, in road-making, and general improvement of land and people, he was equally at home.

The MacLeods have given many eminent men to the ministry, the medical profession, the army, navy and other walks of life. In the medical profession there is no more outstanding figure than the Doctor Ban, and his name is a household word to this day. A very early recollection of the writer was witnessing two old women talking of him, while the tears streamed down their cheeks, lamenting the death of their benefactor. Although he was too young at the time to attach much importance to the talk, in after years he fully realised how much it meant to these women, and to the people of Skye and Uist.

Dr MacLeod was born in North Uist in 1788. His ancestors were settled in Rigg, Skye, and he was a direct descendant of Alexander V of Raasay. His father, Dr Murdoch MacLeod of Kilpheadar, served as an army surgeon in the American War of Independence, and married Mary, daughter of MacLean of Boreray. Alexander was the fifth son of that marriage. He was educated at the parish school and pursued his medical studies in Edinburgh. He qualified in 1809 and succeeded his father in medical practice in North Uist.

His fame as a doctor spread, and as there was no regular medical practice in the island, patients came from near and far, so that his house at Kilpheadar resembled a hospital, as was remarked by a resident of that time. He carried on medical practice in North Uist until about 1825. His brother, Dr Murdoch MD, practised his profession in the West Indies. A brother, John, served as a surgeon in the English Militia, and Dr Donald of Hawick retired after fifty years of service in that Border town. This was a family of doctors and many of their descendants continue in the profession to this day. The Doctor Ban's sister married Rev. John MacIver of Kilmuir, Skye, and, like her father, possessed in a great measure practical medical knowledge, which was a great asset to her husband's parishioners and others. She had great faith in the curative qualities of the many herbs which grew in abundance all over Skye, the efficacy of which the writer experienced more than once. But these are neglected nowadays. Another sister, Flora, returned from America on the same ship as her famous namesake, the deliverer of Prince Charlie, and witnessed the battle with the French privateer, during which the other Flora broke her arm.

The Doctor Ban had great faith in the health-giving properties of shellfish and dulse. As Mary MacPherson, the Skye poetess, has it:

Ach cuimhnichibh, a luchd mo gràidh,
Comhairlean an Dotair Bhàin,
Thugaibh pailteas as an tràigh,
Is deanabh cal air deanntaig.

But remember my loved ones,
The advice of the Doctor Ban.
Take plenty from the seashore,
And make soup of nettles.

'Anns an earrach an uair a bhios a' chaora caol, bithidh am maorach reamhar.' ('In spring when the sheep is lean, the shellfish are fat.')

Dr MacLeod married in 1815 Mary, daughter of Kenneth Campbell of Strond by his wife Anne, daughter of Donald MacLeod of Berneray. They had a family of two sons and four daughters.

As well as practising his profession, he was factor to Mrs MacLean of Boreray and Grimasay. He inaugurated improvements on these estates, which revealed his engineering skill and practical knowledge of land management. He rented the farm of Kilpheadar, and built a house there, which he occupied until the death of his brother Murdoch, when he moved to Baile-an-Loin. This was about 1820. Lord MacDonald, who then owned North Uist, was so struck with the knowledge and accomplishments of Dr MacLeod, that he gave him the appointment of chamberlain of his estates. This involved his living in Portree, where he was about 1829. He remained there until Lord MacDonald's death six years later, when he returned to Uist.

He lived on his farm of Baile-an-Loin, and practised his profession. In or about 1840, he was appointed as factor to the estates of Colonel Gordon of Cluny, Benbecula, South Uist, and Barra. On Colonel Gordon's death he returned to his practice in Uist until about 1851, when he was again to Portree, this time as doctor. Three years later, at the urgent request of the then Lord MacDonald, he took over the medical practices of Strath, Sleat, and Knoydart on the mainland. His first visit to Knoydart was on 12 April 1854, when he went to visit a shepherd's wife, across a wild moor. On his return in the darkness, he lost his way, fell over a precipice sixty feet high, and sustained such injuries that he must have died at once. His body was found two days later and he was buried in the churchyard of Kilmuir of North Uist.

Dr Keith MacDonald, of Ord, wrote many years afterwards, 'What a gloom it cast over the parish of Sleat. The occurrence made such a vivid impression on me, that I remember to this day; it was at 8 p.m. we heard the sorrowful news at Ord.' That gloom was widely felt all over Skye and the Uists. His life was spent in relieving suffering humanity, and sacrificed in the end in that pursuit.

A factor on a Highland estate has not usually been a popular personage, but the Doctor Ban was an outstanding exception. In his *History of the MacLeods*, Alexander MacKenzie, 'The Clach', whose sympathies were all with the crofters and the people, says: 'The Doctor Ban was probably the most popular man who ever acted in that capacity in the Highlands.' A correspondent wrote to his grandson: 'No man knew the people better than your grandfather. He understood their powers, and better still their weaknesses. He knew their capabilities, and how to apply them; a man who knew what he wanted done, and straightway proceeded to carry it out. A man of surprising activities of mind and body, he infused much of his own energy of mind and body into others.'

Dr Ban's engineering knowledge was put to good effect in South and North Uist, beneficial alike to landlord and tenant. In both places, not only are there vast and numerous fresh-water lakes, but the coast is indented by narrow arms of the sea, penetrating far inland, but dry at low water. He conceived a method of closing these sea rivers, by erecting dams of his own invention at several places and restoring the enclosed area to agricultural land which, in time, produced excellent crops of barley, oats and potatoes, as well as pasture. Several fresh-water lakes were drained, and further areas of arable land and pasture blossomed forth, from what were waterlogged swamps. The disappearance of the lakes and narrow inlets made practicable the construction of roads leading north to south and linking east to west.

One arduous undertaking was the draining of Loch Scolpaig, which contained Dun Scolpaig, formerly represented only by a tuft of grass amid waters of the loch. The doctor had a bet with a gentleman visitor that he would drain the loch and erect a tower on the site of the *dun* (earthwork or castle). He set men to work, and won his bet. A cross was unearthed by the workmen, and erected on a pedestal inscribed:

This ancient cross, found in the old graveyard of Kipheadar, was erected on this pedestal by Alexander MacLeod, the Doctair Bàn, of Balelone, 1830–1840.

A tablet was later inserted and inscribed:

This tablet was inserted, and the pedestal was repaired by his grandson, Major Norman MacLeod of Calcutta, 1913–1914.

His work in draining and embanking in North Uist in 1829 gained him the recognition of the Highland Society, who presented him with a handsome pair of branched silver candlesticks.

Tower at Portree

The reclamation of the *machairs* (sand-dunes) serves as a permanent monument to the skill and ingenuity of Dr MacLeod. On the west side of Uist, there were miles of sandy waste, unproductive drifting sand. The idea of putting this waste area to productive use appealed to him, but the financing of the work was a problem. The crofters were deeply in arrears of rent as a result of crop failure. Here was labour to benefit them, and help them to pay off their arrears to the landlords, as well as providing increased pasturage. Two methods were employed. Where the sand was loose, he planted 'bent' (marram) grass, which grows only in sand. The spreading roots of this grass formed a network, which firmly binds the sand together. This 'bent' grass is reaped and harvested in the usual way, and is a valuable material for making thatch. Plaited and twisted, it can be worked into mats, ropes, stools, hassocks, chairs, and horse collars. In the process of time, the consolidation of the sand by the 'bent' roots made it stable enough to grow other grasses and clovers. The 'bent', besides solidifying, gave a certain amount of shelter to the other plants, and the desert became arable. Seaweed, which is in abundance on these western coasts, is a peculiarly suitable manure. The seaweed extracts moisture from the air, and in dry seasons supplies sufficient moisture to nourish the plants.

The other method was of planting turf, from the inland grasslands, in small patches. This can only be practised on fairly solid sand, but is more rapid as the patches soon spread, to increase the ground cover. The reclaimed lands, known as *machairs*, are the richest and most fertile parts of Uist. The ground is soft and elastic to the tread, and the herbage a most refreshing green. Dr MacLeod also advised the planting of iris flags in marshy ground in order to consolidate it.

Between these islands the sea recedes at low-water, and the passage can be made across on foot. There are pools and channels of sea left which are fordable at some places, but dangerous at others. In foggy weather, even the most familiar with these routes cross at great personal risk, for once the route is missed there is little hope for the wayfarer. To guide travellers by daylight, the Doctor Ban erected guide posts to the fords, in the shape of strong stone pillars, with guide boards on each. These were of little use in the darkness. But the ingenuity of the doctor was equal to this. He caused piles of stones to be accumulated on each side of the fords, and two rows of stones to be laid, leading out from the shore, a few yards apart. Travellers were enjoined to carry a stone from the heaps and plant it on either side of the broad path, in line with the last stone out. As the tides flowed and ebbed, a black patch of seaweed was soon attached to each stone. Thus, travellers could follow the path across the fords in the dark, guided by the dark lines of seaweed on each side.

He laid out the hill above Portree Pier to be a pleasure garden, planting flowers and flowering shrubs, and built a tower intending it to be a museum. At Portree he set about building bathing huts, which he hoped would be attractive to tourists, but that project was never completed.

When Doctor MacLeod was Lord MacDonald's factor in Portree, he found the crofters in severe rent arrears, again because of bad harvests. He never harboured a thought of eviction, but looked about for remedial measures to benefit both tenant and proprietor. Loch Chalum Chille in Mogstad was partly but unsuccessfully drained in 1715, and again in 1760. He set men to work, and eventually finished the work with a running outlet to the sea. In a few years, the swamp produced luxuriant crops of hay, the like of which was nowhere seen on Skye. He then tackled Loch Mialt on the Staffin side. But in this he was confounded. After sinking several pits, he encountered solid rock, the excavated material consisting of petrified shells. He constructed a road from Score Gate to Duntulm, a difficult undertaking when one considers the present road.

The works of Dr MacLeod, professional and otherwise, have been a lasting memory through the generations. While acting as factor, he never charged fees for medical services. He was always followed by a crowd when he visited the outer islands. A Barra woman, likening him to Our Saviour, said to a grand-daughter, 'Great multitudes followed him, and he healed them all.'

He was not devoid of humour. He was called to visit a patient who took to his bed from some nervous affliction. The doctor at once grasped the situation: 'Yes,' he said, 'you are very ill, there is a long period of suffering and pain in store for you. I can do nothing for you. I can't bear that you should suffer, I'll just put an end to your pain.' Saying so, he grasped a loaded gun from its rest. The afflicted man bounded out of bed, effectually cured. Another patient, in a depression, could not be helped by any medication. The doctor gave her a bottle of coloured water, to be sucked through the stem of a pipe. She did so and was cured! He diagnosed another old lady as suffering from indigestion, indolence and the excessive drinking of black tea. He ordered her to drink a bowl of milk, sitting on a large stone in front of the house. Afterwards she was to climb the steep Carrachrom, 400 feet above, and facing east inhale ten deep breaths. The same to be repeated night and morning and 'no tea'. She attributed her 'cure' to the breaths from the east.

A grandson of the Doctor Ban and a friend were returning from prospecting for gold in the Australian bush. Weary and hungry, they entered a wayside hostelry for food and rest for the night. Having supplied them, the host noticed they were conversing in Gaelic. When he discovered to whom he was speaking his delight was unbounded and he would not take a penny piece from any relative of the Doctor Ban, or any friend of his, however long they chose to stay.

'S o'n a dh'fhalbh an Dotair Bàn,
Cha bhi duil againn gu bràth,
Ri fear sheasas dhuinn 'na àit,
Ach 's math am plàsd a chainnt dhuinn.

Since the fair Doctor departed,
We will never again expect,
Anyone to fill his place,
But his words are good medicine for us.
   Mary MacPherson

3 SCORRYBREAC

Scorrybreac has been closely associated with the *crodh sith* (fairy cattle). The *crodh sith* came across from Raasay to graze on the bladderwort and the green succulent grass on the seashore slopes of Scorrybreac. When seen, earth from a churchyard was thrown between them and the sea. This prevented their return. The call of the fairies could not penetrate the sacred barrier of sepulchral mould. They became a valuable addition to the herds of the island, and, their return being effectually cut off, the *crodh sith* became assimilated with the native stock!

The Nicolsons or MacNicols are undoubtedly one of the oldest, if not the oldest clan, that occupied Skye. The name is frequently met with in Norway and the Orkney Islands and shows Norwegian origin. The following extracts are from an article published in *Scottish Country Life* in 1918, and entitled 'Clan MacNicol and its Chiefs':

Skene identifies the Clan MacNicol with the region in the north west of Scotland, now known as Edrachaolais, Durness, and Assynt, and declares that, 'the most ancient Gaelic clan which can be traced as inhabiting these districts is the Clan Nicol or MacNicols'.

In the article on Assynt, in the Statistical Account of Scotland, the Rev. William MacKenzie records that:

'Tradition and even documents declare it was a forest of the ancient Thanes of Sutherland. One of the Prime Thanes gave Assynt over in vassalage to one Mackrycul, who in ancient times held the coast of Coygeach, that part presently called Ullapool. The Thane made Assynt over in this manner, as Mackrycul had recovered a great number of cattle, carried off from Sutherland by foreign invaders. Mackrycul is reputed by the people here to be the potent man of whom are descended the MacNicols or Nicolsons.'

According to the Gaelic genealogical manuscript of 1450, in which Skene found so much writing regarding the clans, this account is probably correct, for in that manuscript the descent of the Clan MacNicol is traced in a direct line to a certain Krycul, obviously the Krycul of the tradition. As the letters 'r' and 'n' are interchangeable in Gaelic, it can easily be seen how MacKrycul became MacNicol or Nicolson. The recovery of the great herd of Sutherland cattle from the Norwegian invaders is believed to have been accomplished by MacKrycul, Coygeach, some time in the twelfth century. To accomplish such a feat he must have been at the head of a considerable army or clan. So the probability is that the race of Krycul had been chiefs at Ullapool for a long period before that. This would take their ancestry back to the days of Malcolm Canmore at least. On the death of the last MacNicol of Coygeach, Assynt, Edrachaolais, and Durinish, the chiefship of the clan had, by patriarchal law, passed to the nearest male heir of the race, and the seat of their line was afterwards removed to Scorrybreac, a beautiful spot on the coast of Skye, near Portree. Here they appear to have shown their piety, prevision, or ostentation by benefactions to the religious house, of which the ruins may yet be seen on an island, at the head of Loch Snizort. A small chapel on the south of the building is still known as MacNicol's aisle, and within is to be seen the effigy of a warrior, in conical helmet, and long quilted coat, who must have been a man of much consequence in his time.

The Nicolsons of Scorrybreac: Alexander, 9th head, followed in direct succession by Donald, 10th, Malcolm, Rev. Donald, Malcolm, John, Malcolm, Donald, Norman, John, Norman, and Norman Alexander. Reverend Donald, 12th, died 1698. He had twenty-three or twenty-five children. John, 18th, left Scorrybreac and settled in Tasmania, where the line of succession was continued by the nineteenth and twentieth heads, Norman, and Norman Alexander.

The last Nicolson who lived and died at Scorrybreac was Donald Nicolson, who married Margaret MacDonald of Scalpay. He had four sons and one daughter, who married the Rev. Alexander Nicolson of Barra. This daughter was the mother of Mrs Angus Martin, and grandmother of Nicol Martin of Glendale. Three sons were officers in the Indian Army, and died young and unmarried. The eldest son, Norman, on his father's death, went to Tasmania, where he was drowned. He was succeeded by his brother, John, who married and had two sons and a daughter. Norman, the eldest son and head of the family, married and had a family of sons and daughters. His brother, Edward Reginald, also married and had two or three sons and a daughter. All live in Tasmania.

Donald Nicolson was succeeded by a Mr MacLachlan. The earliest tenant the writer remembers was William MacLeod, who married a daughter of Mr MacLachlan, and succeeded the latter in the farm. Employing a manager, with a high rent, falling prices, and increasing working outlays, Mr MacLeod was compelled to relinquish the farm. He emigrated to New Zealand.

The last Nicolson of the race whom I met was the late Sheriff Nicolson, the Celt of Parliament House, a perfervid lover of Skye. I last saw the genial burly gentleman at the local sitting of the Crofter Commission where, at his request, I acted temporarily as interpreter. His father was Malcolm Nicolson of the Nicolsons of Scorrybreac. He possessed the estate of Husabost, which he sold to Dr Nicol Martin.

Sheriff Nicolson was born at Husabost, 27 September 1827, and died in Edinburgh, 12 January 1893. Once at Greenock (I think) he was sentencing a man for a cowardly and brutal assault, and told him he was such that he would like to have five minutes in a corner with him. Skye is the poorer today since the patriotic kindly Alick Husabost passed the bourne.

Norman Nicolson, Tormad Scorrybreac, was an inveterate poacher. His uncle and the local estate officials failed to make him desist. At last an edict came from Edinburgh, banishing him from the estate, and he had forthwith to go, and emigrated to Tasmania. In his bitterness he composed the following song, which was a popular favourite at all festive gatherings in my early days:

'S gànn gu'n dirich mi chaoidh,
Dh' ionnsuidh frith ard a' mhunaidh,
'S gann gu'n dirich mi chaoidh,

Tha mo ghunna caol air meirgeadh,
Cha teid mi do'n t-seilg leis tuille.
'S gann, etc.

Theid a chrochadh air na tairngnean,
'S cha b'e sin leam aitè-fuirich.
'S gann etc.

'S iomadh latha sgith a bhà mi,
'Nam shuidhe leis 's e lan air tulaich.
'S gann, etc.

Gabhail seallaidh air na sleibhtean,
Far am bi na feidh a' fuireach.
'S gann, etc.

'S tric a mharbh mi fiadh nan stuc-bheann,
Air mo ghluin 's mi lubadh m' uilinn.
'S gann, etc.

Mur a bhitheadh bratheir mo mhàthar,
Dh' fhagainn damh nan ard is fuil air.
'S gann, etc.

Thug na h-uachdrain uainn le ceilg,
An t-saorsa sheilg bh' againn uile.
'S gann, etc.

Cul mo laimh ri laghan fiar,
Tha toirmeasg biadh thug Dia do'n duine.
'S gann, etc.

It is unlikely that I will ever climb again,
To the high forest of the hills.
It is unlikely etc.

My slender gun has rusted,
And I will never go to hunt with it again.

It will be hung on the nails,
And that is no place for it to remain.

Many a day I was weary,
Sitting with it loaded on a knoll.

Casting my eye on the mountains,
Where the deer are wont to dwell.

Often have I killed the stag of the peaks,
On my knee with elbow bent.

Were it not for my maternal uncle,
I would leave the stag of the heights blooded.

The landlords took from us by guile,
The hunting rights we all had.

The back of my hand to unjust laws,
That forbid the food God gave to man.

4 THE ROAD NORTH

By the seashore, about four miles from Portree, is Prince Charlie's cave, to which he was conducted on parting with Kingsburgh and Flora MacDonald, and from which he was ferried across to Raasay, where, under the protection of Mac'ille Chaluim (MacLeod of Raasay), he lay hid in a hut near Dun Cann. One day a traveller was espied making his way towards this refuge. The prince's companions were discussing whether to shoot the intruder. The prince intervened, but one of MacLeod's men retorted that though he was the king, they were the parliament. The wayfarer, disguised as a pedlar, was one of his friends. Captain Malcolm MacLeod arranged to guide him to the MacKinnon country, from whence he reached Moidart, and ultimately France.

The wayfarer passes the reservoir which supplied Portree with water, progressing from the old Tobar-an-t-srup ('Well of the Spout'), where the *cailleachan* (old women) used to meet, and, while the pitchers were filling, discuss the gossip of the day, and the scandal also, too often giving vent to their differences. Two miles out from Portree a magnificent view of the Coolins can be had, the serrated peaks showing clearly against the southern horizon. On the left we have Beinn a' Chearcaill, so called from the several terraces of rock that encircle the mountain. It is separated from the Storr by the Bealach Mor and Bealach Beag, which are both passes to Snizort; the former can be ridden over. The parish minister of Snizort frequently rode over this *bealach* (mountain pass) to minister to this part of the parish. It is now unnecessary, as there are none to minister to. The last visit was made by Rev. Malcolm MacLeod, father of the noted Maighsteir Ruaraidh. The district, though belonging to the parishes of Portree and Snizort, now forms part of the *quoad-sacra* parish of Stensholl. The Storr is the most conspicuous of the mountain ranges. It is little less than 3,000 feet high. The vast solitude, crag upon crag, black frowning precipices, and the oppressive loneliness fill the awe-stricken observers with a weird and eerie feeling, as if expectant of some apparition of the spirits of the past, said to have occupied the caves and rocks of this unrelieved solitude. To the west the rampart decreases till it reaches Bealach Mor, where the ascent is easy, over the Leac an Stoirr of Mrs Macpherson's famous song, 'Nuair bha mi og' ('When I was Young').

Under the rounded top rises the Old Man of Storr. From its base it is 160 feet high, visibly inclining outward, seeming 'as if an infant's touch could urge its headlong passage down the verge'. The Storr was years ago the haunts of the golden eagle. It was a magnificent sight to see the noble birds, with their fledged offspring, swoop and circle in the high heavens overhead. The last pair nesting in Trotternish were in the Quiraing. But now Quiraing knows the king of birds no more. The district between the mountain's base and the lochs is Tote-a-Rom. It was early cleared of the population to make room for sheep, *na caoraich mhor*. The introduction of Cheviot sheep brought an influx of Border shepherds – Dickson, Douglas, Hume, Helm, Brown, Lockhart, etc. Some of these names we still have.

Old man of Storr

Ill fares that land, to hastening ills a prey,
Where wealth accumulates and men decay.

There is but one house, barely visible, in this vast solitude, occupied by
a shepherd.

Caoraich mhòr 's ciobair Gallda air gach beinn is slios is allt,
an aite nan laoch dh'imich do dhuthaich chein.

Big [Cheviot] sheep and Lowland shepherd on each hill, dale,
and stream in place of the warriors who departed to distant lands.

Sheep were of more importance than a contented peasantry, peopling
the straths and glens. It is hoped the Great War has shattered for ever this
unfortunate policy. On the right are Loch Fada and Loch Leathann,
stocked with fish similar to the famous Loch Leven trout, game fighters.
Over sixty-five years ago the writer often fished the lochs, and two or three
hours, with favourable conditions, was sufficient to fill the basket. Later,
forty years ago, with the kind permission of Mr Donald Stewart, the then
tenant of the farm, I got this privilege again. On one occasion, when
returning by the Bealach Beag, I came across a small dark tarn. On the

bank lay the tail of a fish which would have been one of five or six pounds. I loosened my rod and whipped the loch for half an hour, but not a movement. As I was putting up my rod my attention was drawn to a commotion on the far side. I concluded it was the otter which had eaten the fish, and which must have been taken from the lochs below. Relating my experience on my return to an old woman, she became very excited and declared that the tarn was the home of the *each-uisge* (water horse) of Tote-a-Rom. I was sufficiently impressed at the time to give it in future a wide berth. These lochs are now stictly preserved and are the domain of the privileged few. 'Ach a nis tha maor is lann air gach alltan agus ob, chan eil saorsa sruth mam beann anns a' ghleann 'san robh mi og.' ('But now the bailiff and the watcher are on estuary and stream; there's not the freedom of the mountain rill in the glen where I was young.')

Behind the lochs is Ermishadder, with one solitary dwelling, occupied by a shepherd. There are numerous places over Skye with the affix *shadder*, with prefixes such as *cani, mari, elli, anni, culi*. *Shadder, shiadar*, and other forms, mean shieling. The eastern face of the Storr is even more striking than the southern, with a labyrinth of knolls and rocks, intricate and perplexing with Coire-an-t-seasgaich and Coire Scamadale, depressing downward to Bealach a' Chuirn, which is one of the passes to Kensaleyre. The Carn is such a place that a slip might land the explorer out of sight. Beyond the *bealach* is Hartival, a summit not much less in height than the Storr, with the Coire Faoin between it and the Carn Liath.

On the coast are the hamlets of Holm, Bereraig, Rigg, and Tote, once with a teeming population, evicted gradually to make room for sheep. It is said there were forty crofters and eighty cottars, and that when the cock crowed in Tote, the crowing was continued through Rigg and Bereraig, to Holm. The people evicted emigrated, principally to the Carolinas, where many of their descendants are still domiciled. In the corner of an old garden at Holm, I came across a gooseberry bush. Either it or its reproduction must have been over 150 years old, silent testimony among the ruined buildings to the existence of a vanished race. Who can describe the poignancy of mind of these exiles as they turned for a last look at their beloved homes. What a tragedy! And the savage brutality of 'man's inhumanity to man'.

Opposite Holm is the small island of the same name, the resort and nesting place of hundreds of sea fowl. Fire a shot, and one could hardly conceive that the dense cloud could all obtain a foothold on the limited surface. Bereraig has also its ruined enclosures. Here boring for oil was carried out some years ago. Oil was found, but not in a paying quantity. The shore is rich in fossils, and is worthy of a visit from the geologist. When the present road was being made, a cave or underground abode was brought to light. This was built with slabs of stone, and similarly roofed. It was explored to fifty yards – not to the end. It contained the remains of prehistoric animals – at least animals not now known locally. The place was always known as Carn nam Bodach, and was the reputed lurking shelter of the dangerous criminals of bygone ages.

Rigg lies in a hollow, and the numerous population of the past is now represented by a solitary shepherd's house. In the Rigg hollow is the graveyard of the Holm to Tote community. What feelings are awakened on contemplating this God's acre, amidst a desolate waste! A graveyard overgrown with nettles, and a people non-existent. 'Tha'n aitean comhnuidh falamh, fas, air cnamh 'nan laraich luim, is dh' fhalbh na laoich.' ('Their habitations are decayed to bare ruins and the heroes are gone.') Yes. From these sods, bedewed with filial tears, where sleep the ancient sires, the whole population were thrust furth their homes to a land they knew not of, the ruined homes overgrown with nettles, bearing testimony to the ruthless spoiler.

Some years ago a shepherd boy at Rigg thrust his hand into a rabbit burrow, and instead of bunny, took out two claymores, relics of the Disarming Act of 1747, when the Highlanders in most instances gave up old and useless arms, concealing the serviceable, hoping perhaps in more propitious times to draw again the sword for Royal Charlie. The attitude of the chiefs of Skye was repugnant to their people, and henceforth the bond between chief and clan was effectually severed. Many of the clansmen, MacDonalds and MacLeods, scorning the part taken by their chiefs, were out as Jacobites in *Bliadhna Thearlaich*, as the Forty-five is even today termed. Had the Skye chiefs joined, the prince's adventure might have had a different ending. Culloden's disaster was brought about by the incapacity of the leaders in giving battle to Cumberland with his artillery, instead of taking to the mountain fastnesses, and wearing out the royal forces by opportune raids, warfare which the prince's army was peculiarly adapted to carry out. The obnoxious butcher was given an opportunity to gratify his cruelty and lust in this, the only battle which he had won. The claymores passed to the late Captain William Stewart of Ensay, whose brother, Mr Donald Stewart, was the then tenant of the farm.

On the left there is Beinn a' Chapuill (Chapel Hill), separated from Sgurr a' mhadaidh-ruaidh (Fox's Rock) by Bealach Luarsgart, an Airigh Mhor, and am Baca Ruadh (Russet Ridge). Sgurr a' mhadaidh-ruaidh is even more arresting than the Storr. The fox is not yet extinct in the neighbourhood of the Sgurr, and it is difficult to believe Reynard will ever be, with such a sanctuary as Carn Liath 'n Stoirr. Up to seventy years ago, the *brocair* with his pack of hounds was a familiar sight all over Skye, putting up for several days at each farm house. Old Myles Macinnes was the last of his calling.

The rock-bound coast is fantastically penetrated with caves and underground openings. In several parts the land lies over the sea, on a limestone formation, supported by huge isolated pillars, formed by countless ages of sea action. It is altogether a forbidding and dangerous coast, made more so by sharp-pointed submerged rocks, called *na fuamhairean* (giants). In the clefts and shelves colonies of gulls and green cormorants nest. While the gulls sit placidly as the boats pass, the cormorants stretch their necks, glancing from side to side, as if apprehending danger from behind as well as in front, ending in a plunge and dive underneath.

In the distance may be seen Rona Island, rugged and forbidding in appearance. From Rona many years ago the Scorrybreac and other crofters brought boat loads of shell sand to sharpen and fertilise their crofts. In more recent years parties went there for supplies of long heather for making heather rope. Coir yarn and wire netting have taken the place of these. In Rona it has been averred that the unscrupulous stole their neighbours' soil to deepen their own. The population has mostly migrated to Raasay.

In dry seasons the Ronites were obliged to come to Skye for supplies of fresh water. A Mr MacRae and a neighbour, with two servant girls from Rona, were returning from Skye. In the darkness they missed the harbour entrance. The boat was dashed to pieces on the rocks, and the occupants lost. Mrs MacRae (Bean Rona) afterwards kept a lighted lamp as a guide to the harbour. This she kept up for many years, until the present lighthouse was built, and Bean Rona was given a pension of £40 a year from the Admiralty for her devoted unselfish service. Bean Rona afterwards went to reside in Braes, where several of her descendants are settled; the proprietor of the sawmill at Portree is a grandson. Mrs MacRae belonged to a Kilmuir family of good social standing. Her sister, Bean

Cnocowe, was the wife of Roaghnall Ruadh, whose ancestors farmed Cnocowe for many generations. He was a kinsman of Uisdean Mhogstad. But more anon.

As we pass from Rigg to Lealt the mountain range includes the Baca Ruadh, Coire nam Fiadh, Bealach an Eich, Beinn Caiplin, Bealach na Lic, Beinn Edra, Bealach a' Bhor-bhein, Chreag Dhearg, on to Quiraing. A piper, Bruce from Staffin, is alleged to have seen a spectre between Beinn Edra and Bealach a' Bhor-bhein: *colunn gun cheann* (headless body). Bruce is said to have composed the following fragment of a tune and song, while the spectre was disappearing:

'S fhad uam fein bonn Beinn Edra,
'S fhad gun teaganh uam Bealach a' Bhor-bhein.
Cuil nam bruthaichean, bonn nam bealaichean,
Cuil nam bruthaichean, Bealach a' Bhor-bhein.
Dh'fhag mi 'n crodh-laoigh aig bonn Beinn Edra,
Dh' fhag mi na laoigh aig Bealach a' Bhor-bhein.
          Cuil nam, etc.

Far from me the foot of Beinn Edra,
Far from me Bealach a' Bhor-Bheinn.
Back of the slopes, foot of the passes,
Back of the slopes Bealach a' Bhor Bheinn.
I left the milk cows at the foot of Beinn Edra,
I left the calves at Bealach a' Bhor Bheinn.

This is all I have been able to glean. The late Mr Murdo Nicolson of Lonfern informed me that he and a friend came to a mining camp in Victoria, Australia, to rest for the night. He was startled to hear the song and tune above given, ringing out in the midst of miners of all nations. He sought out the singer, who was the son of Am Maor Beag, who was once in Staffin. Mr Nicolson and his friend were next day held up by the notorious Kelly gang, and relieved of their gold.

The west side of the range slopes, the east side is bold and precipitous. Below the higher peaks are the old-time sheilings – Airigh Mhor, Airigh Neill, Airigh Dhonnchaidh, etc. At the foot of these hills are several lochs – Lieurvay, Loch Quire, Loch Dursco, Corcasdale, Clep, all good trouting lochs, especially Lieurvay. On the right are high cliffs bordering on the sea.

The discoverer of iron ore in Raasay found strong traces of the same in Tote, which may yet in more prosperous times be explored.

Lealt Bridge is the north limit of Scorrybreac Farm, twelve miles long and about three miles broad, once cleared for sheep, and now restored to crofters, but in diminished numbers. Upper and Lower Tote was the last clearance of Scorrybreac, which is said to have been carried out at the insistence of a Nicolson of Scorrybreac, grand-uncle of the last occupant of Lonfern. There are many old tales of robbery and murder on Scorrybreac Moor, and it is just such a place as would attract the evilly disposed. There were, perhaps, two or three actual crimes, but the leading facts in most of these, in which a pedlar was the central figure, prove that they are probably variations of the same tale. I shall mention only one. Two brothers, MacDonalds, from Lochaber, of doubtful repute, were shepherds or cattle herds. They had a servant lad from Snizort, on the west side of the hills. The men murdered a packman, appropriated his pack, and threw his body into a gully, since and now called Sloc a' Cheannaiche. The servant came to know of it. The criminals forced him to swear he would tell no living man. To prevent his escape he slept between the brothers. The lad was in terror. One night while the criminals were in a deep sleep, he rose and, almost naked, fled over the hills, pursued shortly after by the brothers until in sight of houses. The lad, in an exhausted state, collapsed at the door of Snizort manse. When he recovered, he was questioned by the minister, but refused to answer, saying he had sworn to tell no living man. 'Well, then,' said the minister, 'tell it to that stone.' He did so, and the minister, who was in a position to hear his confession, took immediate steps to bring the criminals to justice. Such is one of the many tales of Scorrybreac Moor, in which the pedlar is always the central figure. Were but half the number of pedlars said to be killed true, a heavy toll of the travelling fraternity was taken. The murder of pedlar James Orr is on record.

The Lealt River descends in a series of waterfalls to the sea. What a waste of electric power is in the different waterfalls hereabout. Here a disused tramway runs to Loch Cuithir, where diatomite works, employing twenty to thirty men, were carried on for many years, until German competition killed the unscientific methods of production in use. There is a wide area of the deposit, thirty or forty acres in extent, and boring to forty feet did not exhaust the depth. Five miles further north there is another deposit. The material when dried is pure white. It is an effective non-conductor, and when mixed with cement makes the best fireproof walls and flooring. It is the finest material of its kind known, and is well worthy of the attention of builders and insurance companies. Canada has recently begun extensive works with every prospect of success, and where Canadian enterprise and Canadian engineers succeed, it lies with British grit to overcome the obstacles of Loch Cuitheir and provide this country with a material of incalculable value to many industries.

Rigg was famous for a family of MacQueens, who played an important part in the past history of Skye. They were reputed of muscular proportions, and given a wide berth in quarrels. Alasdair Og, mac na Caillich, one of these MacQueens, after a strenuous struggle, overcame in a wrestling bout an Irish champion. Before the latter could be got to a doctor, he died, and was buried at Rudha an Eireannaich (Irishman's Point) near Broadford. There is a Lon an Eireannach in Snizort. The origin of the name is the following. An Irish pedlar procured lodgings for the night in a house at Garalapin. After retiring he became aware of earnest whispering by the inmates. Listening intently he gathered that they were planning his murder. They were intending to slaughter the *eibhrionnach* (castrated he-goat) and not the identically-sounding *Eireannach* (Irishman). Terror-stricken he fled from the house. In this haste and in the darkness he fell into a burn and was drowned.

On the seashore, a mile further north from Rigg, there is a curious huge boulder. It is about 40 feet in height with a circumference of 120 feet. A wide arch penetrates through its centre. Nearby is a similar but smaller one. The former goes by the name An Eaglais Bhreige (Lying Church), and the latter a' Chubaid (Satan's Seat).

Tradition suggests pagan rites being carried out at the Eaglais Bhreige, at which his Satanic Majesty presided. Black cats were roasted alive as one of the sacrifices. A young MacQueen woman is said to have been inveigled to their rites. Her whereabouts became known to her people, who assembled and put to rout the idolatrous assemblage, rescued the young woman and removed the *cubaid*, to where it now stands. Above the Eaglais is the Grianan, a green sunny delightful stretch near the cliff's edge, with Dun Grianan about the centre, and Lon an t-Sithein skirting it till it joins the Lealt. There is a rhyme about Clann 'Ic Cuithein, who performed these pagan rites:

Clann 'Ic Cuithein dhubh man briag,
Clann 'Ic Cuithein dhubh an t-sodail,
Clann 'Ic Mhanainn dhubh na braide,
Ged nach b'fhaid' iad na cas biadaig'.

Black Clan MacCuithen of the lies,
Black Clan MacCuithen of the flattery,
Black Clan Macmhannan of the theft,
Though as short as a dagger haft.

Upper and Lower Tote were cleared a few years after 1800. On a recent occasion, I revisited the old homesteads of Upper and Lower Tote, which were cleared of men to make room for sheep. In these old times, the tacksman or gentleman farmer rented a considerable extent of land from the superior. The major part of this was sublet to subtenants or cottars. In the old feudal times, the tacksman was bound to supply a certain number of armed men for military service with the chief. This number varied according to the extent of the tacksman's holding. The sub-tenants, besides tilling their own portion and paying rent, helped to work their superior's part. The superior had thus a double interest in preserving the number of cottars on his holding.

In Upper Tote, there is one ruin of considerable size, evidently the residence of the tacksman and his immediate servants. Clustering round this main building are the ruins of the subtenants' homes, overgrown with moss, bracken, and nettles. The whole seemed to be within a radius of 120 yards. In Upper Tote I found fourteen such ruins. Five or six of these were obviously dwelling houses, while the others seemed to be byres, barns or sheep cotes. So in these humble homes, within hail and hourly intercourse, there lived these people with simple lives, undisturbed by outside conflicts, bound together by bonds of affection, which conduced to community of interests and enterprise. Though humble their lot, what wonder that they were lovingly attached to the hamlets, in which they, and their forbears for centuries, lived as one family, sharing each other's joys, and mourning together over their sorrows. Periods of sufficiency and periods of hardship might, and probably did, intervene. Yet they bore their lot with patience, and independence of spirit, sadly lacking in our day. These hamlets were self-contained communities. We can well imagine the wrench of the separation that tore their heartstrings when the dread mandate went forth that uprooted them from the land they loved, and the hamlets and homes sacred to them, and their forbears, and from the ashes of their kindred, resting in the *clachan* in the hollow. No wonder at the aged mother's cry, 'O, mo bhron, mo bhron, fuiling a chridhe 's na sgain.' ('Oh my sorrow, my sorrow, suffer, oh heart, but do not break.') Humble those homes may have been, they were the only homes they knew, where they were born and reared, and where they hoped, in the fulness of time, to be laid in the mould, to sleep till the dawn, beside the loved ones gone before. Yes, it was their home. What cared the spoilers? They were encumbrances on the land that was theirs by every moral right.

Lower Tote is much the same, but the ruined buildings are more concentrated. There is no actual march between the two. Where marches were erected elsewhere they were turf dykes, running zig-zag. It is difficult to understand why the *bodachs* (old men) of old built them in this manner, with fifty per cent more labour – perhaps with the idea of more shelter. Lower Tote lies within a radius of eighty yards. How these people spent their lives may be gathered from the well-marked old fallow rigs, seemingly in parts to be tilled in common. These rigs frequently radiate to a centre, at which the present-day crofter would look doubly askance before tackling it. Yet these people, with their crooked spades, tilled and gathered the soil into these rounded ridges. It can be seen, from the mode of tillage, that the crooked spade was the best implement for their manner of cultivation. From these rigs, crops sufficient for their frugal needs were reaped. These hamlets, like many other similar hamlets, were self-containing. All the requirements of food and clothing were produced. For clothing there was the wool from the sheep. This the women folk, and often the men, teased, carded, and spun into yarn. When this was dyed it was ready for the weaver. The weaving and waulking were done in the hamlet. Dyes from different plants and lichen growing on boulders gave a variety of colours. From boulders, a lichen is obtained giving a dye called crotal-a russet dye. A curious belief in connection with crotal is that a man who falls into the sea, wearing stockings or a jersey of this dye russet, sinks like a stone, and does not rise again. And many instances of this fatality of the crotal are given, and firmly believed in. True it is that fishermen avoid anything dyed from crotal, or even approaching it in colour. For linen requirements, patches of flax were grown, and duly manufactured into the finished article. Every hamlet had its own *poit-dhath* (dye-pot). Potatoes, oats, and barley were grown, and these with milk and eggs constituted their standard of living. Each community had its own *brath* (quern). The sea-shore provided a variety in the form of shellfish; working from small boats, or from rocks, fish was, for the most part, abundantly available, supplemented by fresh water lochs and streams.

These hamlets were cleared about 1810. In the interstice of one of the walls, a clay pipe was found, which the old *bodach*, after his last puff in bed, had stuck in the wall. Snuff was not therefore exclusively used. This reminds me of an old relative of seventy years, who, having similarly lost his pipe, was so annoyed that he never after smoked a pipe, nor used snuff, to both of which he was strongly addicted. It is a curious happening that a direct descendant of the MacLean, who was evicted from Upper Tote, over a hundred years ago, should be given, by lot, the land held by his ancestor. The tenant evicted from Lower Tote was John Campbell, married to Catherine, daughter of Ronald MacDonald of Cnocowe, Kilmuir. They must have been of good standing in those days. The writer's family possess a set of silver teaspoons, with their initials, which belonged to them and a china breadplate; also an octagon-shaped china teapot, which belonged to Mrs Campbell's mother and which must be at least 160 years old. There were also a cup and saucer, which belonged to Flora MacDonald, which a friend took away and failed to return. The sub-tenants of Lower Tote shared the same fate. A few got holdings in the vicinity and the old churchyard at Rigg occasionally receives kindred dust. The son of one of the evicted had gone to Glasgow, where he built up a considerable business. Family troubles and business worries unhinged his mind, and he returned to Skye and ultimately back to the scenes of his former life. It was pathetic to see old Neil wandering among the old familiar surroundings, and imagination may conjure the bitter, elusive thoughts passing through the perturbed mind, when in place of the old homesteads he found a silent desolate waste, peopled by sheep.

In a small glade beside Upper Tote is Tot-nic-Fhionnlaigh, where the notorious *shebeener* of Rigg, referred to elsewhere, ended her sordid life, having been expelled from Rigg, but allowed to settle there among the MacLean cottars.

Ruaraidh Mor, who was a cotter in Tote, went to Portree market and sold a beast, intending to bring home half a boll meal (70 lb). Finding there was none in the village, he set out for Broadford, got his supply, and physically carried it home a distance of thirty-six miles. Another old man, whom I knew, told me he had gone to Sconser for two stones of meal, a distance of twenty-four miles. The stone of these days was 17½ lb. It is not to be inferred from this that poverty was the general condition. Except in exceptionally bad seasons the population had sufficient food to supply their frugal wants. Rory Mor's son, an old man, who was three years when evicted from Tote, took a very active part in the land agitation.

To the north of Tote is the hamlet of Lealt; certain districts of old went under special cognomens: *na sgairbh* (cormorants) of Lealt, *coin* (dogs) of Trotternish, *eireagan* (pullets) of Sleat, *moganaich* (footless stockings) of Durinish, *faochagan* (whelks) of Strath, *saoithein* (saithe) of Raasay, *boguis* (bugs) of Digg, *na cait* (cats) of Waternish. A saying attributed to Raasay people is: 'Bu mhath an sgadan nuair nach faighte an saoithein.' ('Herring is welcome when saithe is not to be had.') These were all taken in good part. The MacLeods long coveted the rich corn lands of Trotternish. Barred in this, in contempt they described it as *duthaich na stapaig* (meal mixed with cream).

Bealach Mor and Tot-a-Rom, it is said, were long infested with robbers, until advancing justice and mutual protection compelled them to seek more secluded quarters. One, MacRaing, had made himself especially obnoxious. The cave mentioned, Carn nam Bodach, may have been his lurking place. The heap of stones and turf over the cave gave its name long before it was discovered. It may have been given that name by people seeing MacRaing or his followers haunting its vicinity. MacRaing disappeared, and later was heard of in the Coolins.

We arrive at the old house of Lonfern, whose walls are over five feet thick and thatched; it is presumably in the same condition as it was in the past centuries. For several centuries the Nicolsons, cadets of the Scorrybreac Nicolsons, occupied this small farm, son succeeding father, down through the ages. They were a cadet branch of the Nicolsons of Scorrybreac. The main line dates beyond the days of Malcolm Canmore, and are now in Tasmania, where the direct succession has been carried on through the generations since John, the last occupier, left Scorrybreac.

A long lease of Lonfern expired in 1811. The tenant of that time was Donald Nicolson, born about 1728, although several Nicolsons had succeeded one another before then. In a letter, dated from Lonfern on 18 March 1811, to Lord MacDonald's factor, Donald Nicolson requested a continuation of his lease, mentioning that he was now eighty-three years of age. The request for a renewal of the lease was duly granted and the succession went on unbroken. Indeed it is recorded that in the sixteenth century Lord MacDonald offered the Mrs Nicolson of that day Lonfern free of rent 'co fhad's a bhuaileas tonn air traigh, no bhitheas bainne geal aig bo dhuibh' ('while a wave strikes the shore, or a black cow has white milk'). When the offshoot from the main line took place is perhaps wrapt in the estate archives. Perhaps the claymores found hidden some years ago were once wielded by Nicolsons.

This Donald Nicolson, the writer of the above-mentioned letter, was succeeded by his son Donald, who married Janet Nicolson of the Scorrybreac family. She long survived her husband. She was very old and the writer was very young when he saw her. She was a lady of exceptional charm of manner, and of proverbial hospitality, as was the house of Lonfern throughout the ages. A number of years after Donald's succession and death, owing to a succession of unfortunate circumstances, the tenancy was being renounced, and preparations made for the disposal of the stock, when the unexpected happened in the form of a draft for £700 from the eldest son, Murdo, in Australia, and the occupancy was preserved.

The family of Donald Nicolson, and his wife Janet, consisted of five sons and two daughters: (1) Murdo, married without issue; (2) James, unmarried, went to Australia; (3) Donald, married with issue; (4) Malcolm, unmarried; (5) Godfrey, unmarried; (1) Kate, married with issue, one son and two daughters; (2) Mary, married with issue.

While there are members of the female side at home and abroad, the male line is extinct. The last of this long line died in 1905. There are several descendants of the female side in the colonies, from one of whom the writer recently received a letter. Thus came to an end the long line of the Nicolsons of Lonfern. Murdo was the last occupier and died in 1910, aged eighty-seven. Mrs Nicolson died as late as 1871 or thereabout, at an age between ninety and ninety-five. At the graveside the late Mr John Stewart of Ensay referred to the deceased lady, and the family to which she belonged, in words of unstinted praise.

Lonfern was a small farm, rented at £25. There were four cottars, each paying £3. The cottars of Lonfern were coeval with the tacksman, their forbears occupying for centuries. The cottars were removed. Some got refuge with friends, who divided their meagre holdings to accommodate their landless relatives. Thus subdivision set in with disastrous results. The rent of Lonfern was raised from £25 to £80, and the crofters' rents proportionally. This was the last straw, and could have no other result than revolt of the crofters. It is but just to mention that this was at the instance of a new proprietor of the estate. The struggle for land reform followed. The 'fair' rents fixed by the Land Court are in many cases still higher than Lord MacDonald's rents.

After his parting with Prince Charlie, MacDonald of Kingsburgh, afterwards arrested, was in hiding for a time in Lonfern. Sir Archibald Geikie, on his geological survey in Skye, spent more than a week in the old house, and was hospitably entertained by the lady of the house. He was termed by the natives *bodach nan clach* (old man of the stones). A son was sent to Portree with his specimens in a pack-saddle, to which he was adding on the way. It is difficult for the older generation to conceive of Lonfern without a Nicolson. Lonfern, or Alderburn, points to at least an alder wood in the past, and roots of the alder are found in the adjoining peat moss. Jutting out from Lonfern is Rudha nam Braithrean (Brothers' Point). On the highest part, approached by a narrow saddle of land, are the remains of a *dun*. When built, and by whom, is hidden in the distant mysteries of the past. Its foundations give indication of the strength of the building material used. Here, tradition tells, lived Donald MacDubh Ruaraidh and his brothers, noted reivers. When the MacDonalds and the MacLeods were at feud, Donald observed neutrality, until he saw which side was likely to win. He then joined the winning side, partaking of whatever booty was to be had. On the cliff side of the old fort there is a deep opening, called Preas Dhomhnuill Dhuibh (Black Donald's Cupboard), where the wily reiver stored his booty. Excavation from above would show whether there was a connection between the fort and the *preas*.

Across Brothers' Point runs a natural basaltic causeway. This I have been told appears in Flodigarry, and reappears in Kilmuir. There is another, if not a continuation, showing in the face of the Boreraig cliff, descending into the sea, thereafter continuing under the sea. The line fishermen avoid this vicinity, fearing their lines will become entangled in it. Locally it is called the Saothair.

Once I passed a night with an old friend in Bracadale many years ago. The cakes at breakfast were in the stook the night before. The grain was partly burnt in a large pot, then winnowed and dried in the pot, always turned over with a large wooden spoon, till hard and dry. The grain was ground in the *brath* (quern), sifted and ready for use. This meal was called *min ururaidh*. A bowl of beaten cream with two spoonfuls of *min uruaraidh* was a dish fit for a lord. When mills were erected the people were thirled (constrained) to these so that the multure would support the mill. As always with a primitive people, they were loath to change, and clung to the *brath*. An edict was given that anyone using or possessing a *brath* would be evicted. Eviction was the terror of those days. It took years before it was finally out of use. There is a cave by the seashore in Valtos called Uamh nam Brath, where these were concealed. The writer has one which he found as *acairs* (anchors) on a 'black' house, with upper stone, however, broken in two. One woman operated the mill, and another fed the grain. 'Two women shall be grinding at a mill, one shall be taken, etc.' It is not a remote recollection to remember seven mills in Trotternish, and sufficient meal was made for the families, with often a surplus to sell. Romisdale was the last in working order, and there has been no grain ground there since 1915. It is the same all over Skye.

A story, or tradition, related to me sixty years ago, was recalled to me recently by hearing it anew. At Bearn Dun Dearg in Valtos, two large blackbirds were seen fiercely fighting, till nightfall put a stop to it. The following day two funeral parties met at the spot. As neither party would give way, they laid down their burdens and began to fight for the passage. The fight was long, and much blood was shed before either of the combatants gave way. Ultimately one gained ascendancy, took up their burden, and resumed their journey. The person who related this to me vouched for its truth. 'Nach b'aineolach na daoine bha ann 'san am sin,' remarked an old man, not doubting its truth. In the olden days funeral rites were frequently disgraced by drunken revelry, though the tale related above seems improbable.

Iomair na Cailleich lies at the base of Creag Dhubh Chuithir. It is a green sward of considerable extent, and shows unmistakable evidence of cultivation, which is striking testimony to the change of climate. The *cailleach* (old woman) is supposed to have been one of the MacQueens, who lived in Rigg. She was an amazonian virago, named Kate MacQueen, living in Marrishadder. On account of her quarrelsome and pugnacious disposition she was banished by the community. She took up her abode near Loch Cuithir, cultivated that piece of land, and with fish from the loch sustained a precarious existance. When pressed, she would cross the hills, and make exactions on the dwellers there. The Martins and their dependants were for two days trying to catch a refractory filly. On the second day they so encircled the animal that there was but one avenue of escape. Martin saw Cailleach Chuithir in the distance, and shouted, 'Cheit Mhor, a nighean mo pheathar, coinnich an loth.' ('Big Kate, daughter of my sister, meet the filly.') With long sweeping strides Ceit threw herself into the fray, caught the filly by the neck, twisted it on its back, and held it down till it was secured with a *taod gaoisid* (halter). For her exploit Ceit Mhor's delinquencies were forgiven, and she was readmitted to the community.

Though I have not come across tales of illicit distilling in Skye except one, there is no doubt such existed. On the mainland seizures are periodically made. Quite a number of years ago, a seizure was made at Kintail, and the whole outfit carried to Kyleakin. The smugglers followed, broke open the place of custody, and carried off their property. An old Trotternish friend of my early days, a native of Kintail, then resident at Kyleakin, was arrested on suspicion of having guided the smugglers, and lodged in prison. In court, proof of guilt was lacking, and Alasdair Piobair was set free. Some years after, I met him and he admitted the charge. Poor Alasdair has long since crossed the bourne.

The following is an amusing account of the only one of which I heard. From various happenings a house in Maligar was suspected. When operations were in being, scouts watched for a possible surprise approach. Hastily returning, they reported the gaugers were *en route*. A Mrs Ross took the situation in hand. The men were ordered away when the gaugers appeared. The whole incriminating apparatus was laid on the floor, covered with a bolster and blankets, on which a woman lay down, simulating child-birth. The train was all laid, when the gaugers entered. What they saw made them retreat hastily. They did not return. The illicit work continued and the township was afterwards fined £5 by the estate.

The following are the fragments of a song relating to the episode:

Ho! gur laglach na mnathan,
Nuair a ghabh iad air bearraid an Righ.
Deoch slainte nam mnathan bha 'm Malaigear,
Chumadh na gaidsearan dhinn.

Nuair thainig na gaidsearan 'n bhaile,
Gu'n d'thug iad earraid bho'n Righ;
Bha dearrsadh 'nan claidheamhnan geala,
'S ghabh fir an taoibh Sear romhpa fiamh.

Bha Bean Ian 'ic Coinnich ri h-asaid,
'S i gu mor ag gearan a cinn;
Bha te aig a ceann 's te' aig a casan,
Is poca math braiche r'a druim!

O, gu bheil bean aig an Rosach,
Is dhuraichdinn botul 'na broinn,
Le a cuaile de bhata math daraich,
Gu bhualadh air carraig an cinn.

Oh, how amiable the women,
When they hoodwinked the king.
A health to the women of Maligir,
Who would protect us from the gaugers.

When the gaugers came to the village,
They brought the king's equipment;
There was a shine on their bright swords,
And the men of the east side took fright from them.

The wife of John, son of Kenneth was in labour,
And sorely complaining of headache;
One attending her head, and one her feet,
And a good bag of malt at her back!

What a wife Ross has,
I would wish her drink a bottle,
And a good oak cudgel,
To belabour the crowns of their heads.

Though the illicit still was not much in evidence in Trotternish, the *shebeen* sixty or seventy years ago was common, but the activities of the excise have stamped out this evil. There was an old *cailleach*, called Nighinn Nic Fhionnlaigh, living at Rigg, before that part of Scorrybreac was wholly cleared. She kept, as it is called today, a *shebeen*. It was a half-way house for those going and coming between East Trotternish and Portree. On one occasion a party of six left their homes on a Tuesday to pay their rents at Portree. As usual Nic Fhionnlaigh's half-way house was visited. The *bodachs* made a longer stay than they intended. They became helpless to proceed or return. By and by, as each arose from his drunken sleep, he took his cloak and returned home till all were gone except one, Iain MacDhomhnuill Bhain. Iain also started; now and again he picked up a cloak dropped by his companions, till, by the time he reached home on Sunday evening, he was carrying six cloaks!

Passing on to Valtos, we are in the cradle of the land agitation. Not since the days of the fiery cross was such a military force seen in Skye as when 250 Royal Marines paraded in Staffin, accompanied by a number of drafted police. Norman Stewart, the Skye Parnell, was arrested. The leader in charge made a technical mistake, and Stewart, on the advice of a Glasgow solicitor, sued for damages, and was awarded £25 and costs. The soldiers and the drafted police were on the most friendly terms with the people, and organised concerts to relieve the monotony of their own existence, and amuse their neighbours. The local leaders (of whom only two now remain) considered the battle won with the advent of the military, and counselled law abiding thenceforth, which accounts for the few arrests in this district in comparison with other parts of Skye.

In the front of Valtos school is erected a memorial commemorating the sacrifice made by old pupils. The memorial was unveiled by Nicol Martin of Glendale, whose forebears belonged to the district. An old ruin nearby was the school in which the Martins of Marrishadder got the elements of their education. The school was a Gaelic one, taught by Iain Ruadh Mac an Aba, grandfather of the late Mr John MacNab of Kilmuir School. Mr MacNab possessed higher acquirements than usual in these schools, and the young Martins benefited thereby in their English studies.

A prominent feature of the landscape is Dun Dearg, with a sheer drop of 300 feet to the sea. Dun Dearg was said to be one of a series of *duns* round Trotternish on which fires were lit, calling the clansmen forth. The call to battle was last given in 1745, when the MacLeods mustered 1,100 and the MacDonalds 1,200. When told they were not going to fight for Charlie, only 500 of the MacLeods took up arms and the MacDonald chief fared no better.

In the peat mosses of Valtos several bronze spearheads were found, and a barrel, formed from the hollowed trunk of a tree, filled with what appeared to be tallow, was found embedded in the moss. The police took possession of the barrel. There were also found several neatly constructed brown vases containing flint arrowheads. The finder declared they were *saighdean sith* (fairy arrows), strengthened, in his belief, by their being found in Cnoc an t-Sithein, (fairy knoll) in Ellishadder. The writer saw them with the late Mr Urquhart of Staffin School, but further trace was lost.

Opposite Valtos is the Carraig Mhor, rising to a height of 600 feet, with a perpendicular drop to the sea. It descends to the outlet of Loch Mialt, then rises to the same height on to Staffin Bay, without a break except the Cabhsair. Under the higher ridge is Carnach-a-Roimh. That, together with Carn Mor in Culnancnoc, is second only in weird desolation to Carn Liath an Stoirr, and has resulted from the action of countless ages of ice and water.

The Cabhsair is a paved pathway from the sea, through a depression in the ridge, constructed by the famine committee in 1846. The range embraces the famous Kilt Rock, so called because of its formation resembling kilt pleats. The outlet of Loch Mialt, the Steall, has a drop of 400 feet. Loch Mialt is a wide sheet of water, and in it is a species of fish called alpine char, which I am assured is found nowhere else in Britain, except in one of the Cumberland lakes. In appearance it resembles a sea trout, with a somewhat elongated tail, silver scales, and red soft flesh. The specimens I have seen ranged to the size of a small herring, but one caught a number of years ago weighed three pounds. It is not very palatable. Brown trout were introduced several times, but did not thrive. From the north side juts out Rudha na Ceardaich (Smithy Point). The smithy at one time was surrounded by water. Here the clan smith fashioned his sword blades, secure from prying eyes on his tempering process. The once resounding smithy is replaced by the prosaic sheep-fank. An attempt was once made to drain the loch, but rock baffled success. It would be easy today, and a valuable extent of arable and grazing land would result. Probably one should prefer the picturesque loch to remain. Dun Raisburgh rises above the loch.

There is a persistent tradition that the East Trotternish was deeply wooded until relatively recent times. This belief is strengthened by the remains of huge tree roots found deeply embedded in the peat mosses and acorns are often turned up, showing that the oak flourished in distant times. With many of the old people, this belief is a certainty. In a letter received from an old friend in Australia, the following occurs: 'When my great-grandfather's great-grandfather, Angus Nicolson, Marishadder, used to visit his son in Grealine (a mile distant), he could only see the sky above him at one spot for the density of the wood. When the cows were let out in the morning, they were not seen till they came home for their calves at *trath eadraidh* (milking time).'

Out-stack and the Kilt Rock, Staffin Bay, Skye

A mile westwards, over the moor from Dun Raisburgh, is the original home of the Martins of Marrishadder, and not far off is Clachan 'ille Mhartuinn (Kilmartin), the burying-place of the Martins. The tomb of the Martins in Kilmartin churchyard bears the following inscription:

The Tomb of
The Martins of Marrishadder

This stone was erected by Dr MacGregor of Duntulm, Melbourne, Australia, in affectionate remembrance of his beloved mother, Abigail MacKenzie Martin, wife of the late John MacGregor, who died in 1839, aged forty years. 'A good woman is better than precious ointment, and day of death than the day of one's birth' (Eccles. 7:1). Also of his much-beloved uncle, Martin Martin of Duntulm and Tote, who died in 1874, aged ninety-two years. 'With long life will I satisfy Him, and show Him my salvation' (Ps. 91:16). Also of his much-beloved Aunt Isabella, wife of Martin Martin of Tote, and grand-daughter of MacLeod of Raasay, who died in 1852, aged seventy-two years. 'For she had been a succourer of many and myself' (Rom. 16:2). Also of his dear beloved cousin, Alexander Martin, banker, Portree, who died in 1872, aged twenty-nine years. 'When we were yet without strength, Christ died for the ungodly' (Rom.5:6).

There are a considerable number of Martins in the district. The present head of the family is Captain Nicol Martin, the genial laird of Glendale.

A Peninsular War veteran was buried in Kilmartin many years ago. Fifty years after, his son was buried in the same grave. In excavating the grave a bullet was found which the old soldier had carried in his thigh from the battle of Toulouse till his death, and which had not prevented him from taking part at Waterloo.

5 A TRAGEDY

In the year 1812 a boat, with nineteen persons, was returning from Portree to Culnancnoc. The boat was overladen, and one man and two women went ashore at Lealt. A number of others made to land, but when taunted with cowardice they kept their places. The boat was still overladen with men and goods. In the darkness the heavily-laden boat struck the Dubh-sgeir, near Brothers' Point, within a mile of their destination, capsized, and all the occupants were lost. The upturned boat was driven to the Gairloch shore, and the only body recovered was found in the boat, his hands locked round one of the thwarts. It is recorded that all the dogs in the vicinity kept howling all night. Nearly every family in the township lost one or two members. *Bathadh na Dubh-sgeir* (the Drowning at Dubh-sgeir) is spoken of even today with poignant feeling. The following is part of a song or lament composed at the time by a resident of Raasay, one MacLeod. It was taken down from a man ninety years old:

'S bochd an naidheachd, 's gur bronach,
A tha ann an Tròndairnis thall.
Gu'm bi mi caoidh fhad's is beo mi,
Mo luchd eòlais a bha ann.

'S gu'm be sud na fir bhoidheach,
Nach robh gòrach mu'n dram;
Bha gu socair, ciuin, steòrnal,
Modhail, eòlach, gun mheang.

'S ann an caolas na Dubh-sgeir,
Thuit na suinn bu ghlan dreach.
Dh' aithnich' an cuideachd righ iad,
An deidh na miltean a thoirt as,
Gur e neart bh' anns a' ghaoith,
A chur bhur n'inntinn a' beachd.
B'e meud an luchd bha 'na broinn
Chuir do'n ghrunnd sibh air fad.

Ach a Mhurchaidh Mhic Leòid,
Bu tu oigfhear mo ghràidh,
'S mi gu'n aithnicheadh do gheòla,
Ruith le seol chun a' bhàigh;
'S mi ri fadadh an teine,
Do ghillean suairce mo ghràidh,
Ged nach bitheadh de m' chinneadh,
'S ann leam bu duilich do bhàs.

Ach a dheagh Mhic 'illeathain,
A bhuail an t-saighead gu dan,
'S tu a chaill na fir-thighe,
Nach robh r'a fhaighinn na b'fhearr;
Chaill thu t'aire 's do shugradh,
'S beag do shunnd ri ceol-gair',
Gus an cairear 'san uir thu,
Do shlat 'g urachadh dhuit craidh.

Ach a Dhomhnuill Mhic Thormaid,
Thainig shlad earrachail ort dàn,
Cha b'e cumha do chrodh-laoigh,
Chuir do smuaintean fo chràdh,
Ach ri cumha do leoghann,
Bu ghlan fhaoilt am measg chàich;

B'e sud brod na cuid chuideachd,
'S nach robh truideal 'na chàll.

Dhomh'll 'ic Caluim a Steiseal,
C'uim' nach faighnichdinn thu?
Fhir ro mhath am beul na h-oidhche;
Fhuair luchd conneimh dhuit cliu.
Duine ro shuilbhire, fosgarra,
Lamh a chosdadh na cruin,
B'e sud brod an duin-uasail,
'N am dol suas chon a' bhuird.

Ach a Mhor nighean Ruaraidh,
'S culaidh-thruais thu co-dhiu.
Chaill thu pearsa do ghualainn,
D' an robh uaisl' agus cliu;
Do chlann bheag 's iad mu'n teine,
Gun aon ghill' air an triuir.
'S ann leam fhein gur a duilich,
Mar a thilleadh a' chuis.

Bad the news and sad,
That is over in Trotternish,
I will mourn while I live,
My acquaintances who live there.
These were the handsome men,
Who were not foolish in drink;
Who were placid, gentle and prudent,
Courteous, knowledgeable without fault.

It was in the Dubh-sgeir channel,
The comely stalwarts perished.
They would be recognised in a king's company,
After thousands had fled,
It was the strength of the wind,
That confused your minds.
It was the burden of the weight she carried
That sent you to the bottom.

But Murdo MacLeod,
You were my beloved youth,
Well I recognised your boat,
Running under sail into the bay;
And I, kindling a fire,
For my gentle favourite lads,
Even if you had not been of my kin,
Your death would be my sorrow.

But worthy Maclean,
That the arrow struck most keenly,
You indeed lost the household,
Whose better could not be found;
You lost your interest and pleasure,
You have little mood for laughter,
Until you are consigned to earth,
Your havoc awakening the pain.

But Donald, son of Norman,
Spring loss came heavy on you,
It was not lament for your cattle,
That made painful your thoughts,
But mourning your lion,
Who was most welcome among others;
Who was choice among company,
And not quarrelsome in his nature.

Donald, son of Calum, from Stenchol,
Who would not ask for you?
Excellent host at nightfall;
People you met found respect for you.
A frank and cheerful man,
Ready to spend a crown,
That was a perfect gentleman,
When going up to the festive board.

But Marion, daughter of Roderick,
You are indeed an object of pity.

You lost the source of your support,
Who had nobility and reputation;
Your little children are at your fireside,
And not a boy among the three.
Sad it is to me,
How the affair turned out.

One of the two women who landed at Lealt was Oighrig Dhomhnuill 'ic Iain, who lived and died, old and blind, at Valtos in 1883, reputed to be a centenarian. Her brother Peter, who was a Gaelic school teacher, was the only man who left the boat at Lealt.

On the opposite side of Brothers' Point a similar fatality occurred fifty years ago. In that case all the bodies were recovered.

From Culnancnoc a number of emigrants sailed from Uig about 1838. There was another ship, I believe, about 1847. Though not a forced emigration, many of the women shed bitter tears as Culnancnoc faded. 'Cha b'e Cul nan cnoc ach aghaidh na greine,' sobbed one. ('It was not "back of the hills" but the face of the sun.')

There is a Loch Seunt near Quiraing, which of old was considered a holy loch, but has no connection with the loch in the following:

Uisge tobair Teala-breac,
'S duileasg Loch Eun,
Faochagan an Rudha Dhuibh
'S Smalagan an Riadhain.

The water of Teala-breac well,
The dulse of Loch Eun,
The whelks of Rudha Dhuibh,
And the saith of Riadhain.

I suppose the water, the dulse, the whelks, and saithe are of pre-eminent excellence. Loch Eun at any rate is famous for its dulse, and *mathair an duileisg* (mother of dulse), which makes the finest caragen, pleasant to the taste, nourishing, and white as cornflour pudding. This is now neglected, as well as nettle soup and dulse soup, both healthy and nourishing. The people of the olden times made full use of these and other similar foods on land and shore. An eminent doctor told the writer that any person living near the shore should have dulse soup once a week for its medicinal and health-giving properties. I remember people coming from Snizort to Holm for supplies of dulse, a distance of twelve miles. Dulse contains iodine, and before iodine itself was discovered it was considered very efficacious as a sweetener of the blood and warding off or curing scrofulous or glandular afflictions. An Orkney saying is: 'He who eats of the dulse of Guerdie, and drinks of the wells of Kildingie, will escape all maladies except black death.' It is largely eaten raw in the Western Isles. Chopped small and boiled with a bit of butter, some flour, pepper and salt, it makes nourishing food, and pleasant to the taste.

In the hamlet of Breacry, there is a jet of pure sparkling water, gushing through a limestone rock. It is called Tobair a' Bhodaich. In the far-away ages there were a church and graveyard here, Cill Catriona, named presumably, as usual, after the first interment. There is not a vestige of either. The stones of the church were used in building later houses, and in removing these a baptismal font was brought to light. At the time it was thrown aside. It disappeared for many years and was forgotten. Forty years ago it was unearthed by a plough, and restored to its possible original site by the *tobar*. The stone is considerably larger than the usual of these. Who the monk or saint who performed the religious services was, there is no local traditional evidence. The jet of water from the rock is said to have been created, Moses-like, by the saint. There was another *cill*, or rather *caibeal*, 200 yards away, called Caibeal Sine.

A Cill Chatriona thainig mi,
A Caibeal Sine thainig mi.

From Catriona's church I came,
From Sine's chapel I came.

These lines were quoted by the old man who supplied the above, but he could not explain the meaning, if any, in the lines, except that it was an old saying. As the two *cills* were deserted, and interments, possibly re-interments, made to Culnancnoc, in Cill Eoghain, half a mile distant, it may refer to re-interments from the former to the latter.

6 MARRISHADDER

Over a hundred years ago a bridal party crossed the hills to Snizort, where the marriage ceremony was performed by Rev. Malcolm MacLeod, father of Mr Ruaraidh. The party consisted of the bridegroom, two friends, the bride and her sister. On the return journey the bridegroom became ill. He was helped along by his friends, but died beside Loch Corcusdale, above Maligar. The night fell, and it was pitch dark, and, to add to the difficulty, snow and mist obscured all contour of the landscape. It was agreed that the women should proceed to secure help. A swollen stream compelled them to deviate from their destination, so that the lonely watchers by the body despaired of succour. It was agreed that one should remain and the other seek assistance. The latter was Lachlan Martin of Marrishadder. He was the most powerful member of a family noted for strength. The women ultimately arrived safely, but nothing could be done in pitch darkness. There were no lanterns in those days. 'Gun solus lanntair ach ceann an fhoid' ('Without lantern light, but a burning peat'), as Mrs MacPherson has it in her exquisite song. When help reached the lonely watcher, there was no sign of Lachlan Martin. His body was discovered on the bank opposite that from which he started. Seemingly in the darkness he stumbled into the loch. He had, therefore, fought his way through the loch. His boots were full of sand, and his hands clutched tufts of grass. His footprints were discernible in the sandy bottom of the loch. He had died after a terrible struggle. The death of Lachlan Martin, who was a general favourite, and highly respected, was greatly lamented. The one-day bride married again, a man in Earlish, where her descendants are today, while grandchildren of the groomsman are resident in Maligar and Marrishadder. Cairns mark the spots on which both deaths occurred. The following prophecy, attributed to Coineach Odhar, the Brahan Seer, is associated with 'Three stern struggles on the north side of Loch Corcusdal'. The following is a fragment of a lament for Lachlan Martin:

Bho thaobh an Ear Throndairnis,
Dh' fhalbh an comhlan grinn,
Gu dol a dh'ionnsaidh posaidh.
Mar bha ordaicht' anns gach linn,
Gu'n d' thainig sneachd is ceo orra.
Nuair dhorchaich neoil na h-oidhch',

Gu'n d' bhasaich dithis comhladh dhiubh,
'S thug sin bron is deoir bho'r suil.

Tha clann Mhic 'ille Mhartainn
Air an lot mar tha gu trom;
Chan eil aobhar gair' aca.
Thuit a' bhearn gu lar tha lom;
Chraobh a b'aillidh blath,
Bh' anns a' gharadh air a bonn,
Gu'n d' ghearradh i cho trath,
'S dh'fhairich cach gu'n d'rinn i toll.

Gu bheil do mhathair airsneulach,
'S a h-astar air fas mall.
A' smuaineachadh nan cleachdaidhean,
'N am altrum dhi a clann;
Sgeul nach bu mhath le cach.
Bhi 'gan cur a mach roimh 'n am,
Bu tlachdmhor le cinneadh t'athar,
Thu bhi fathast air an ceann.

From the East Side of Trotternish,
Went the elegant company,
Going to a wedding.
But as has been ordained in each age,
Snow and mist overtook them.
When the shades of night closed on them,
Two of them died together,
And this brought sorrow and tears from our eyes.

The family of Martin,
Are already greviously wounded;
They have no cause for joy.
The loss fell on a home that is bereft;
The tree of lovliest bloom,
That stood in the garden,
So early was cut down,
And others felt it left a gap.

Your mother is weary,
And becoming slow of foot.
Remembering the events,
Of the times she nursed her children;
A tale that distressed others.
Their being dispersed before their time,
It would be a delight to your father's seed,
If you were still at their head.

7 TOWNSHIPS AROUND STAFFIN

Carnan Mairi (Mary's Little Cairn) is below Creag Dhubh, south of
Bealach Olasgart. Mary had been in Beinn Choinnich for several weeks
nursing a family. She set out for her bothy in the dusk of the evening.
Though but half a mile distant, she never reached it. Dense mist fell, and
she had wandered on till she fell exhausted. The cairn was erected on the
spot on which the body was found. There is another Carnan Mairi in
Kilmuir. There are many such cairns all over Trotternish, as the practice
was universal to erect a cairn where death outside took place. There is a
stretch of upland above Marrishadder called Grimiscaig, and a river of the
same name joins the Staffin River. In the sides of a waterfall, Bruthach an
Eas, coal of excellent quality is found. The writer personally used a
quantity, and can testify to its quality. Creag Mhic'ille Phadruig is in
Glasbheinn, and a local song is 'Suiridhe na Glasbheinn' ('The Glasbheinn
Courting'). Clach an Leabhair (bookstone) is a prominent object near the
sea shore at Digg, on the west side of Staffin Bay. It is said to have been
used as a desk for his rent book by Donald Gorm when collecting his rents
from his tenants and crofters. Donald Gorm is said to have been mortally
wounded before Eilean Donan Castle, the stronghold of the MacRaes of
Kintail, and his restless spectre, it is said, has long haunted his old castle
of Duntulm.

Beside Dun Raisburgh, overlooking Loch Mialt, there is a huge
stone, Clach an Tuill, flat and smooth on both sides, with a hole
through its centre. The legend is that a Gairloch man put his finger in
the hole, and tossed it across the sound! Weighing tons, it is of
sandstone, and how it came there is a mystery, as there is no sandstone
within miles – probably it was by remote glacier movement. Rudha nan
Con Gorma is on the north side of Staffin Bay, and the legend about

the *coin ghorma* (blue dogs) is as follows. Mac Iain Ghill, on entering his sheiling, found it occupied by a strange, fierce-looking beast. His dogs attacked it, when it spoke, and requested Mac Iain to withdraw his dogs. He refused, and the beast fled, pursued by the dogs. The dogs failed to return, and were found next morning mangled and dead on the Rudha Cnoc a' Chrochaidh. There are several *cnocs* bearing this sinister name, where the 'Laird's' will was done. The execution of Judge Morrison of the Lews, and his three sons, which is perhaps more tradition than fact, may have been the origin of the name. An attempt to hang Black John of Garafad was frustrated by John carrying off, Samson-like, the gallows and all, by supernatural power.

A church once existed at Sartle, dedicated to Saint Maolrubha. The usual graveyard was beside, or contained it, called Cill-Maree. All those *cills* have been walled in recently. An old man described this as a waste of money. 'Does any want to go there, and can anyone there come out?' was his dictum. There are two holy wells near the *cill* (church), Tobar an Domhnuich (Well of Sunday), and Tobar na Slainte (Well of Health). Sithean Thot, or an Sithean (Fairy Knoll) is on the road to Staffin. The fairy revels, it is said, were on a large scale, the men fairies dressed in brown, and the *mnathan sith* in green, capering and dancing furiously, till at the midnight hour the phantom host magically vanished. Dun Borve was another *sithean*. They were very troublesome to a resident there, and he sought counsel of a neighbour, who told him to go and shout, 'Dun Bhuirbh 'na theine!' ('Dun Borve on fire!') The fairies came rushing forth, shouting, 'Beinn Bhuirhb, 'na theine, gun chu gun duine, mo chearslagan snath, 's mo phocannan mine.' ('On fire, without dog or man, my little balls of thread, and baggies of meal.') A man at Digg got all his work done by the Flodigarry fairies. He was at a loss how to get rid of them. A neighbour told him to give them a sieve, and order them to bale the sea. Cnoc an t-Sithein in Ellishadder is another of the many *sitheans* throughout Trotternish. The belief in witchcraft was firmly held by many up to forty years ago. A crofter's wife, going to the peat bank, saw a hare sleeping in a tuft of grass. Quietly and quickly she grabbed it. The hare gave out the unearthly scream peculiar to the animal. The woman threw it down and returned home, and no one could convince her she had not handled a witch.

West of Bealach Olsgart, there is a sheiling called Airigh an Easain, so named from a small waterfall falling over a deep cleft in the rock.

The spot is dark and gloomy, and has always had an ill-omened reputation for ghosts and goblins. It was said a pedlar was murdered here, and that his ghost still haunts the place. Few care to venture alone along in the dark. Many years ago, a Staffin man was overtaken by darkness on his return. As he approached the *eas*, he was horrified to see before him a being of unusual movement zig-zagging the road. He was afraid to proceed, and loath to return. A momentary rift in the darkness showed who it was. 'Is that you, Charles?' he cried. 'It's me,' was the reply. 'May you never be there again,' said the startled traveller. 'May I never,' said Charles. The ghost was a harmless lunatic from near the man's home. Leaving the road, and turning to the right over the moor, you descend into the darkness of Glen Sniosdal, with the sloping Quiraing on the right, and Creag Sniosdal nam Fitheach (ravens) on the left. On the top of the *creag* is Aite Suidhe Fhinn, where it was said one of the Feinne kept vigil for any signs of the approach of the Norse galleys. From his perch on the rock it was said he could have his feet in the loch below. It is a weird solitude. Loch Sniosdal is a repellent-looking loch, lying in a hollow west of Quiraing, on which the sun seldom shines.

When and where the belief in the *each-uisge's* (water-horse or kelpie) existence prevailed, the superstitious could hardly fail to associate this gloomy loch with the monster's abode. The *each-uisge* of Loch Sniosdal frequently appeared as a fascinating gentleman, dressed in immaculate black, with white linen front. A woman, herding on a sheiling, once met him in that guise. They sat down, and he nestled his head on her lap. While stroking his head with her hand, she felt grains of sand in his coal-black hair. She at once knew who it was. Though terror-stricken she remained calm, and showed no signs of fear. After a time her companion fell sound asleep. She then slipped quietly away, and was well on her way to safety before he discovered her absence. The poor woman heard his infuriated neighing behind her, but succeeded in reaching the nearest house, more dead than alive. It was said that the people of hamlets two miles away could hear his enraged roaring.

8 STAFFIN

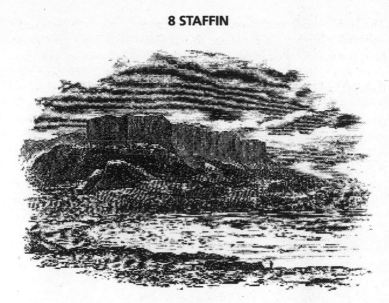

Staffin Bay

In Staffin there are four churches instead of two, within a stone's throw of each other. Pitiful in the extreme are these divisions, and the waste of energy and wealth. Yet this zeal for 'principle' is not marked by more regular church attendance. There is, however, one hopeful feature – all bitterness is gone, and more tolerance is apparent.

Staffin Bridge was the only one of nearly a dozen that withstood the disastrous flood of 1877. Several have been rebuilt a second time since.

In the district are two post offices with telephone service. My recollection goes back to one postman, carrying the mail from Portree to Kilmuir three times a week: Old Iain Posta (as his father Donnchadh Posta before him). There was no service to Staffin. An old woman crossed the moor to Kilmuir once a week and, wrapped in a red handkerchief, brought back what letters there were, which she distributed, receiving twopence for each. Old Iain's work is now done by two motor-cars, ten postmen, and five post offices. The contents of old Effy's handkerchief are now dealt with by a motor-car, two horses, seven postmen and two post offices. Old John was given a post in the Edinburgh Post Office, but the cramped city life did not suit him, and he was soon back to his native hills.

The Royal Mail in Skye

Staffin meal mill, like all the mills in Trotternish, is in ruins, or put to some other use. Up to fifty years ago, and even later, they were kept busy, often night and day, and nearly all meal requirements were met by home production. All over the country there are decaying remains of the old wheels, bleached white, once picturesque in activity, associated with the flash and thunder of the cascade. Without them poetry and art are poorer, and we regret the demise of one of the rural charms of the countryside. Every township had its *atha* (kiln), and kiln-drying of grain was done at night. The *atha* was the rendezvous of the youngsters in the vicinity, who indulged in their youthful pranks. The *bodachs* would be seen with pack-saddle and full rush bags on the way to the mill. Today there is neither *srathair* (pack saddle) nor *plada* (saddle cloth) in the district. The mill that once existed there is gone, the *atha* is a thing of the past. What are the causes of this retrograde movement? There are several, and change of climatic seasons comes first. The snow and frost of the winters are changed to excessive rain, washing the substance out of the soil. The summers have not the ripening warmth, and the harvests are late and cold. Increase of cattle prices, more ploughing and less spade work, and absence of rotation of crops, all these contribute to the decline in crop returns. The ploughing is seldom over four inches deep, resulting often in an impenetrable solidity of ploughpan, remedied only by double ploughing, or by the spade. Since the seasons have become wetter, rotation of crops is absolutely necessary. Seventy per cent of seed oats have usually to be imported, yet in face of this, an official of the Board of Agriculture recently proposed to repair and put the mills in working order.

Another lost industry is weaving. There were quite a number of weavers. The women were busy teasing and carding the wool, and spinning it into thread. When the web was got from the weaver, the waulking was done. Waulking was a great attraction for lads and lassies, who joined in the waulking songs. At the end there was a scramble for the *mnathan luaidh* (waulking girls), each lad endeavouring to get his own favourite to see her home. The *luadh* and *cliath-luaidh* (waulking board) are gone, as well as the old-time *ceilidhs,* where the old-time *bodaich* congregated together, the younger listening, 'nuair a bhiodh gach seanair aosmhor liath ag innseadh sgeulachdan gun gho, air na gaisgich fhearail ghreannmhor bh' anns a' gleann nuair bha iad og.' ('When each grandsire, old and grey, told artless tales of each manly, comely warrior who was in the glen when they were young.') These happy and informative *ceilidhean* are past, and we are the poorer.

Staffin Inn, which is now 'dry', was and still is usually designated An Tigh Ban, from its being the only 'white' house in the district. Staffin Lodge, built sixty-five years ago, was the headquarters of the marines, covered by a warship in the bay. It is amusing to me, as one who took an active part in the land agitation of 1883, to recall the elaborate steps taken by the government to curb the 'rebel' crofters – three warships, a strong contingent of marines, and munitions sufficient to blow Skye into the sky.

Staffin Bay opens to the north-east, and the roar from its surf-beaten boulders can be heard twelve miles distant. Staffin Island partly covers the bay to the east, and Flodigarry Island to the north. An amusing incident, which occurred here some time ago, seemed to show a still-lingering belief in the *each-uisge.* Two men were digging for sand eels on the shore by moonlight. They heard blowing and plunging in the bay. By and by the heads of sea monsters were seen making for the shore. Terror-stricken, the men fled, climbing a precipitous rock, which they would hardly dare risk in daylight. Breathless, they reached home with the terrible tidings of an invasion of sea monsters. The monsters, however, were but the cattle ferried to the island on the previous day by the farmer, and then swimming back to their usual pasture. Staffin Bay is beautiful with its white boulders and sand when calm, but when the north wind blows it is magnificently grand, with its huge rolling waves, and the observer feels how insignificant man is in comparison with the mighty forces of nature. Nearby was the home of Domhnull Saighdear (Soldier Donald), one of the 'Thin Red Line', and Indian Mutiny. Donald was equally at home on land and sea. He was a frequent visitor, and had many thrilling tales to tell. He had sunstroke in India, and sometimes took to wandering. Coming from Portree he kept to the seashore. When his passage was barred, Donald sprang out and swam to the next accessible place.

9 QUIRAING

Quiraing

Towering above is the famous Quiraing, or rather Cuith Fhraing. The 'board' is a wide platform, covered with velvety grass, ideal turf for laying a bowling green. It is 100 feet long and 60 feet wide, surrounded by columnar pillars, rising to a height of 80 feet, as if they were so many gigantic Highlanders ready to defend the entrance to the sacred precincts. It is truly a wonderful assemblage of fantastic nature, bewildering in its confusion, instilling an awesome feeling, expectant of encountering some ghostly phantom, gliding noiselessly through one of the many apertures around. It is said that a ghost appeared at different periods, always making its entrance by the same opening. A smith threw a piece of iron through this cleft, and so laid the ghost. The needle rises to a height of 120 feet. The broken crags and surrounding configuration is equally impressive and confusing. On the south face are three conical 'hillets', rising from the flat on which they stand, in symmetrical beauty, to heights of 80 to 160 feet. Artificially they could not have been more regular in form, and, placed in a maze of lower hillocks, cause all sense of direction to be lost. They are named the Dun Beag, Dun Mor, and the Meirleach. While sheep graze to the top of each, the owners must await their pleasure to come down the steep declivity. Green from base to top, they appear an oasis amid a desert of rocky heathery waste. These, with Quiraing and its surroundings, must have had their origin in the same volcanic upheaval.

Tradition tells us of one *fraing*, who lived hereabouts, who, when danger threatened, as it often did in these days, from Danish invaders, there concealed his cattle. Even if discovered, his few retainers could defend it from any force brought against it. There is an easier route for the more timid, by following the Allt Garbh from Sartle to its source, which is a huge cauldron of bubbling water, pure as crystal, whose very look gives to the weary traveller a sense of refreshened feeling. In the clear water scores of small trout dart hither and thither. Right above this, turn to the left and in a few minutes you are standing on the 'board'. This entrance is rather disappointing until the traveller makes his way further in.

A visit to Quiraing in fine summer weather will be enjoyed by the most fastidious. Being caught there in a storm, however, tries the nerves of most. The mist settles on the top, the whistling wind follows, sweeping forward the settling mist. Drops of rain are the heralds of the coming storm. Tiny tinkles of water soon become so many rushing, foaming streams. The howling of the tempest sweeps through and about those age-old basaltic pillars and precipices. The shrieking wind demon is ear-splitting and blood-curdling and the fast gathering dusk gives an unearthly aspect to the scene, weird to the point of apprehension.

Sixty years ago, during the season, a constant stream of tourists visited Quiraing, often fifty and sixty daily. (Visitors today view it from a passing car, and report they have 'seen' Quiraing.) The 'guide' met them at the *bealach*, and conducted them along a path constructed for the benefit and safety of the visitors. Many notable people visited Quiraing in these days, among whom were Prince Arthur (duke of Connaught), the ex-empress Eugenie, the Prince Imperial and other notabilities. Prince Arthur landed from a yacht in Staffin Bay. The ex-empress was a pathetic figure, with a careworn yet beautiful face; the prince, a tall, spirited young fellow, destined to fall a victim to the Zulu assegais. It fell to the writer's lot to provide part of the imperial luncheon, in the form of a goodly grilse from the Rha, the only fish he had from that stream, while scores were secured from the Conon – how, it does not matter now.

Sartle was one of those farms occupied by retired army officers. Crossing to the westward by Bealach Olasgart we have the southern face of the Quiraing on our right, and the wide stretches of crofter land on our left. Along the road are still seen traces of the cloud-burst of 1877, covering the lower ground with huge boulders, stones and gravel, while the mountain side is scarred and seamed. The Quiraing range depresses gradually to the *bealach*, while on the left rises the rounded form of the Maoladh. From the top of the *bealach* a fascinating panorama is presented. The purpled moor, studded with lochs and scarred by streams, the numerous crofter hamlets nestling here and there, and down to the water's edge, the wide expanse of ocean, hugging in white breakers the shores of Raasay and Rona, showing in contrast its dark rocky outline, the coast of Gairloch and Torridon, with their well-marked hamlets and the huge mountain tops of Wester Ross, showing their serrated peaks against the eastern horizon, making an arresting landscape. Passing on for a mile, a westward view is equally fascinating. In view are the Ascrib Isles, Waternish, and the distant outline of Uist fading midst the mists of the western sky.

Along on the north an inland promontory headland attracts attention, Sron Bhiornal. Tradition tells us that a *nighean righ Lochluinn* (Danish princess) is buried here. Bhiornal became ill on the voyage, and the fleet put into Flodigarry Bay. Before death she requested her father to bury her on this headland, so that she might look out over the sea to watch their coming and going. Such is the old tradition related to me. Blar a' Bhuailte in Kilmuir is the battlefield on which the Norsemen are said to have made their last stand in Skye. The last man, Arco Bronn-mor, fled, and was pursued by a MacSween and slain. For this MacSween got Braes. There is another Leac Nighinn Righ Lochluinn in Rona or Raasay. The legend connected therewith is that the son of the Greek king eloped with Nighean righ Lochluinn. They were followed, and the prince was killed. The princess caused a deep grave to be made. When her lover was put in the grave, she jumped in after him, and a *leac* (slab of rock) was placed over it.

Sgeir or Creag Fhearchair, near Borniskitaig, is named after one Farquhar Beaton, a Kilmuir character, who used to fish from it. The Rev. Alexander MacGregor, 'Sgiathanach' ('the Skyeman'), wrote about Farquhar and gives his daily prayer, which invariably contained the petition, 'Na tuiteadh do ghras oirnn mar an t-uisge air druim a' gheoidh.' ('Let not thy grace fall on us as the water on the goose's back.') The writer recalls an old man to whom was attributed in prayers the petitions:

Cnamhan cogaidh 'is e fad as.
Pris air duine 'is air ainmhidh.

Grumbling of distant war.
A price on man and beast.

10 FLODIGARRY

Flodigarry House, close to the sea-shore, and nestling, sheltered from the north wind, under Eilean a' Chinn Mhoir, is situated among beautiful surroundings. In Mrs Macpherson's song, 'Soraidh le Eilean a' Cheo', she refers to Flodigarry: 'Flodagaraidh sgeimheach c'aite 'eil d'fhiach de ghrunnd.' ('Beautiful Flodigarry, where is your worth of soil?') It is part of the granary of Skye, and perhaps no part exceeds it in fertility. It is opposite Eilean Altivaig, which forms a breakwater to Staffin Bay. On Altivaig there was a chapel dedicated to St Turos. I have heard it called the Spuidsear.

Natives have long maintained that fairy music often issued from a half-concealed heap of stones at Flodigarry. Flodigarry House was built and occupied till recently by the late Major R.L. MacDonald, a direct descendant of Flora MacDonald. His occupancy of the modern house was a connecting link with the occupancy of the old house by the famous heroine. Looking back, we may picture the gentle modest heroine, in the springtime of youth, the newly-wed bride of Allan MacDonald, wandering over the grassy glades of her home. Perhaps the ordeal through which she has passed is occupying her thoughts, contrasting it with the serene peace of her home, with a loving husband, and looking to a future of happiness, quiet and undisturbed. Little thought of the dangers and trials the future had in store for the brave mother and husband. The house has now passed into other hands and is now a well-equipped hotel.

Glendale, in the distant ages, was reckoned one of the four best pasture grounds of the glasgobhair nam Fiann (grey goat of the Fingalians). The other three were Glen Uig, Glen Sgaladail, and Glen Romasdail, and the following ancient rhyme refers to this:

Gleann dail an Diurinnis
Gleann Uig an Trondairnis
Gleann sgiamhach Sgaladail
'S Gleann Aluinn Romasdail.

Glendale in Durinish
Glen Uig in Trotternish
Beautiful Glen Sgaladail
And lovely Glen Romasdail.

11 DUNTULM CASTLE

Passing beyond Flodigarry, in the distance, on an elevation of considerable height, overlooking the sea, portrayed visibly against the azure tint beyond, arise the spectral ruins of Duntulm Castle. How gaunt and weird they appear on the skyline, as if they were the Fionn of world-old ages, keeping watch and ward for the approach, as of old, of the Lochlann galleys, bringing death and ruin in their train. For position, no better could be chosen for a stronghold, requisite in these ancient unruly times. James V anchored his fleet in Score Bay and admired its impregnable position by land and sea. What grim tragedies are associated with these hoary walls! Its present state seems a judgement for the atrocities of the past. One has an eerie feeling going through those halls of the ghostly past. The superstitious may well imagine the ghostly presence which is said to have driven the MacDonalds from their ancient citadel, to take residence and refuge at Mogstad, seven miles south. With the wind whistling and shrieking through these awesome pillars, one cannot but feel that the spectre of Donald Gorm is prowling among his old haunts, and the wail of his victim, Uisdean Mor, seems, in the shrill moaning of the eddying gusts, to be the agonising groans from the dark dungeon underneath. And we leave the awe-inspiring spot with an occasional look over our shoulder, until well outside the grim precincts of Caisteal an Duin. In the vicinity are Cnoc na Comhairle (Hill of Pleas); Cnoc a' Chrochaidh, significant and ill-omened (Hanging Hill); Cnoc a' Mhoid, where justice was administered by the chiefs, the trembling wretches approaching a court where justice was untempered with mercy; Cnoc na Faire, where watch was kept for the approach of enemies by sea or land; and several others. The MacDonalds abandoned Duntulm about 1730. An old drawing, dated 1750, shows the castle still intact. Below the castle there is a low, even, flat ledge, with a deep straight groove, which extends from highwater mark, made by the keels of the galleys when being launched or drawn up.

Duntulm Castle

To the west of the Castle is Uaimh an Oir (Cave of Gold), where, perhaps in the hour of danger, the chief, as did his prototype Mac a' Choiteir at the other end of Trotternish, concealed his gold and valuables. When Donald Gorm Og succeeded his uncle, a valuable paper was missing. The ghost of the latter was seen to frequent the castle, but his nephew failed to intercept him. By the advice of a friend, seven torches were prepared. When the ghostly form was seen to enter, the torches were lighted and the bearers entered. There the old chief and two fellow-ghosts were found drinking in the castle cellar. Donald Gorm indicated where the missing paper was hidden, and it was recovered.

It is told of Black John of Garafad, who carried off the gallows from Cnoc a' Chrochaidh by supernatural means, when about to be hanged, that he had made a compact with his Satanic Majesty to give himself up to his will in a year and a day, for this gift of supernatural power. When the time expired, Satan came to claim his subject. 'There I am,' said Black John, pointing to his shadow. Satan went off with it, and the form of Black John never after cast a shadow.

While tradition invests Duntulm Castle with such shocking tragedies, imagination conjures the barbaric splendour and revelry of the past lords of the Isles.

Ged tha thu 'n diugh a t'aibheas fhuar,
Bha thu uair a d' aros righ.

Though thou art today a ruin cold,
Thou wert once the dwelling of a king.

The MacArthurs, the hereditary pipers, possessed a special dwelling and land. They were highly rated by the chiefs and clan. The hamlet of Hungladder was assigned to them. They taught a piping school in a hollow behind a hill called Cnoc a' Phiobaire (the Piper's Knoll). Many of them are buried in Kilmuir churchyard. There is a memorial stone erected to the memory of one of the MacArthurs in this churchyard. Notwithstanding the ravages of centuries of the contending elements, the lettering can, with patience, be read as follows:

'Here lies the remains of Charles Mackerter, whose fame as an honest man, and remarkable piper, will survive this generation, for his manners were easy and regular as his music and the melody of his fingers will . . .

Here it ends abruptly and unfinished, for whatever reason.

Tot a' Chocaire is near the castle, and presumably the cooking was carried on here. This recalls many similar instances of this in the old days. Most country houses of the better class had their kitchen *dubh*, where the cooking was done. The writer recalls such kitchens.

In about 1616 Donald Gorm fixed Duntulm as the family residence. Duntulm etc. was sold about 1832 to Captain Fraser of Culbockie. The whole purchase forms what was known as the Kilmuir Estate, now belonging to the Board of Agriculture.

At Borniskitaig, tradition says Donald, son of Reginald MacSomerled, cut off his left hand, and threw it ashore. It is said he and a rival raced for the shore, and Donald won by thus casting his hand on the beach. Hence 'Lamb Dhearg Clann Domhnuil' ('Red Hand of Clan Donald'), and 'Air muir 's tir', as the badge or motto of the clan. The latter is more often seen as 'Per mare per terra'. Sir Donald MacDonald XII of Sleat is said to have been the last 'lord' born in Duntulm.

In the Forty-five the MacDonalds and MacLeods took no part, though many of their followers independently joined the prince. MacDonald was persuaded to refrain by his adviser, Martin of Bealoch, and MacDonald's decision would influence the MacLeods. The adhesion of these two clans might have made all the difference between victory and defeat; and from having had some worthless nonentities on the throne.

The farms of Duntulm, Flodigarry, and Sartle were occupied by the late Mr John Stewart of Ensay, the famous breeder of Highland cattle, the progenitors of most herds of Highland cattle today. Mr Stewart was a connection of the Stewarts of Garth, and a splendid specimen of the old Highland gentleman, affable and approachable by every class. In his day, his cattle carried off the chief prizes for whatever classes he put forward at the principal shows. He himself was a familiar and respected figure at these events. Once, when twitted with loss of prizes to his son Donald, the old gentleman pawkily replied, 'Cha sgoiltear an darach ach le geinn dheth fein.' ('The oak is split only by a wedge of itself.') Mr Stewart later took over the large farm of Scorrybreac, succeeded there by his son Donald, now of Lochdubh, Nairn. The connection of the Stewarts with the north began in the Island of Lewis. Archibald Stewart was known as Fear an Eilein Riabhaich. He and an elder brother, Alexander, farmed the extensive grazing farm in Lewis known as Lewis Park (a' Phairc Leodhasach), which came prominently into the limelight by the extensive deer raid by the crofters during the land troubles. The occupancy of the small farm of Scudaburgh was their first connection with Skye, in which Mr John Stewart and his son, Mr Donald Stewart, occupied such commanding positions in Skye farming circles. Scudaburgh was acquired as a landing and resting place for their stock from the Long Island on their way to the southern markets. The elder son of Mr Stewart, the late Captain William Stewart, was invalided from the South African War.

12 FLORA MACDONALD'S EARLY LIFE

Flora MacDonald, Fionnaghall, nighean Raonuill 'ic Aonghas, was born at Milton, South Uist, in 1722, and died at Tigh an Duin near Kingsburgh, Skye, 4 March 1790. Her father, Ronald MacDonald, a cadet of the Clan Ranald family, was tacksman of Milton farm, and her mother, Marion MacDonald, was a daughter of the Rev. Angus MacDonald, parish minister of South Uist. Flora's father, a gentleman farmer, belonged to a class which exercised a powerful influence in feudal times. The farmer was the link between the chief and the people. While the chief lived in dignified affluence in peaceful times, the farmer was more in touch with the daily life of the people who were just tillers of the soil. The chief variety in their lives happened when the fiery cross was sent round.

Flora lost her father while yet a child. The eldest son Angus then succeeded to the farm of Milton. Her mother's second husband was Captain Hugh MacDonald of Armadale: Clann Uisdein, known as Uisdean Cam (One-eyed Hugh). Of this marriage there were, among others, James, who joined the Dutch service, and Annabella, who married Major Alexander MacDonald of Cuidreach. Hugh was reckoned to be the strongest member of his clan. He emigrated to Carolina and died there about 1780.

It was not a genial climate in which Flora had her early upbringing, yet it was one calculated to foster virility of mind and body. The island of Uist is one of a chain of islands, separated by narrow treacherous inlets of sea, and familiarly called the Long Island. It is swept by the wind and waves of the fierce Atlantic, which forbid the growth of trees or even shrubs. The *bent* on the sand dunes and the heather on the uplands maintain their ground only by a strenuous struggle. Yet the Long Island has a strange fascination. It has long stretches of white sands on the western side, against which the Atlantic rollers beat in vain, forming embankments of sand, clothed in short fine vivid green grass, from which unrivalled sunsets can be witnessed.

In such surroundings, amid the sea-scented breezes of the west, and distant from the luxuries and advantages of city life, grew up the simple maiden, whose life sheds lustre on perhaps the darkest and most sombre period in the history of the Highlands. The early stages of her life and education are left a good deal to imagination. But from the state of education and facilities in the Highlands at the time, she must have much lacked the advantages of early training. She was fortunate, however, in being within reach of Nunton, the home of the chief of Clan Ranald, and Lady Clan Ranald, with the keen eye of the specialist, detected strong indications of uncommon qualities of heart and mind in the girl of twelve or thirteen.

She took the warmest interest in Flora, and from that time she seems to have regarded her with the affectionate care of a mother. She took her for a period to her home in Nunton to be educated along with her own daughter; soon the adopted daughter made herself a favourite in the family, by the charm of her winning way. Lady Clan Ranald was in constant touch with Lady MacDonald, wife of Sir Alexander MacDonald, chief of the MacDonalds of Sleat, whose seat was then at Mogstad, in Kilmuir. The friendship and intercourse between these two ladies explain how Flora's education was attended to and how the door opened to her to the higher circles of society. She was not spoiled by being led to these giddy heights, but kept steadily before her her dutiful devotion to her mother and her friends.

The full story of Flora MacDonald's life has never been written, but we get glimpses of her by several writers, and when all are pieced together, we see why the heroine has lived in history, and why succeeding generations have kept her memory green. As Donald Mogstad was the Lochinvar of Skye, she has been the Grace Darling of the Highlands of Scotland. Perhaps the fullest and most satisfactory account of her life is that given by the Rev. Alexander MacGregor, parish minister of Kilmuir, and afterwards of the West Church, Inverness. Both he and his father were much respected ministers in the parish with which the life of Flora MacDonald was so much associated. Mr MacGregor was therefore in a better position than any of his contemporaries to gather and link together the various outstanding incidents in her life as handed down from father to son.

13 THE RESCUE OF THE PRINCE

The outbreak of the war between Great Britain and France in 1743 afforded the heir of the Stewart house an opportunity of attempting to realise the ambition of his life. The French help which had been promised was not given. The prince, impatient of the dilatory promises of the French king, landed in Scotland in the summer of 1745. He resolved to fight his way to the throne, and bent all his energies to gather around him the different Highland clans, and then persuade Scotland to follow him. It was a hazardous attempt, and as subsequent events proved, it ended in complete failure, and brought disaster to the Highlands. Culloden's battle should never have been fought in the face of Cumberland's artillery. The Highland army should have been withdrawn to the hills and guerilla warfare adopted, for which the Highlanders were specially adapted. Flora MacDonald had returned to her brother's house at Milton, when the news of the unfurling of the prince's banner at Glenfinnan reached Uist. Flora, it is said, was not a pronounced Jacobite. Her friend and patron, Sir Alexander MacDonald, was influenced by his adviser, Martin, though himself a strong Jacobite, to hold back, as the promised French guns had not been sent. Scene after scene followed the triumphant march of the prince. One thing became evident – that the nation did not support the prince and all was lost at Culloden. Had the Stewarts taken advantage of the seething indignation of all classes over the massacre of Glencoe, the chances were strong that the nation would have supported them against the authors of that foul crime. There is ample evidence that only the hopelessness of the enterprise, without the promised French support, kept the Skye chiefs back. Their clans to a man would have followed. As it was, many joined the prince. He managed to escape to the west coast and reached Uist. With one or two followers he wandered from place to place. The news of the prince's arrival in Uist became known. The government took immediate steps to capture the prince, and a price of £30,000 was put on his head. Though he was known to hundreds, no one claimed it. 'Tho' £30,000 pounds they gie, yet there are nane that wad betray.' He was hemmed in by land and sea. Then came the incidents which ennobled the name of Flora MacDonald. It seemed to her at first that for a simple maiden to pull the prince out of peril, when his enemies were closing around him, was an impossible piece of work. Yet her heart was human. Lady Clan Ranald was eager to help. The fact of Flora's mother being in Skye seemed to suggest the only way by which to get the prince to a place of safety. It was strategy to save life. It was not disloyalty to the reigning monarchy that moved the heroine to devise means for safety. Her religious convictions in no way hampered her compassion to one who was hunted and ready to perish. It was under these circumstances that Flora left her home, accompanied by Neil MacEachan, to meet Lady Clan Ranald, to devise means to get the prince to Skye. Flora and her attendant were arrested in crossing the ford between South Uist and Benbecula, and kept in confinement until the arrival of the superior officer. That officer proved to be her step-father, Captain Hugh MacDonald of Sleat. She was not only set free, but also given a passport for both herself, Neil MacEachan and 'Betty Burke, an Irish spinning maid'. To make more certain, her step-father gave her a letter to her mother to the effect that he was sending home her daughter Flora, accompanied by Betty Burke, an Irish spinning maid.

Prince Charlie's cave

After some preliminary arrangements with the prince, Flora, Lady Clan Ranald and Neil MacEachan arrived at the hut in which he lived. Her presence was the brightest incident in the itinerary of the unfortunate prince. He readily fell in with the proposal to act the part of the Irish maid, and being provided with suitable clothing, he stepped on board the open boat which was to carry him over the sea to Skye. All danger was not however passed. As the six-oared boat passed out of the creek, sloops of war were espied in the open sea. They passed south, and the boat at midnight started on the long voyage to Skye. In the early morning the wind died away, and there was a dead calm. Troops on land noticed them off Waternish Point and signalled them to come alongside. The boatmen disregarded the signal and the soldiers opened fire, and several shots passed harmlessly over the boat. Flora encouraged the men to pull hard and they were soon beyond range, while the sloop lay becalmed. They landed between Uig and Mogstad in Kilmuir, at a point since called Rudha Phrionnsa (Prince's Point). When the danger was passed the prince became more cheerful and sang snatches of songs. Mogstad was not far off, and Flora knew Lady Margaret was friendly, but as a precaution she told the prince she would leave him there and survey the land, and it was well she took this prudent step. She was warmly greeted by Lady Margaret. She was introduced to Lieutenant MacLeod, who was in charge of troops in the north of Skye. He eagerly questioned her about the prince, but she warded off suspicion of any complicity in his affairs. She was on her way to Armadale to see her mother, and just called at Mogstad. Flora disclosed the matter to Lady Margaret, who was greatly alarmed for the safety of the fugitive. Sir Alexander was not at home, but his factor, MacDonald of Kingsburgh, was in the house, and she despatched him with food and refreshments to the prince. Kingsburgh then left, accompanied by the Irish maid. Flora, accompanied by her attendant, took another route from Mogstad, but joined the prince's party before reaching Kingsburgh.

Much curiosity was aroused by the tall awkward woman who accompanied the factor. On crossing a stream the prince let his skirts trail in the water, and Kingsburgh warned him of the suspicion it might arouse. At a further crossing he tucked his skirt higher than necessary. At this crossing they were met by a party of local military, ostensibly in search of him. One of them knew the prince, and with a significant glance at Kingsburgh, said, 'O Mhorag, nach tu dh'fhas mi-bhanail bho'n urraidh.' ('Oh Marion, how unmaidenly you have become since last year.') Two miles from Kingsburgh is Tobar a' Phrionnsa (Prince's Spring), where, it is said, the party rested, so that darkness might envelop their arrival. Kingsburgh entered with his three guests; Mrs MacDonald was aroused. After an ample repast the prince slept long and soundly. Next day the party left, Kingsburgh and the prince (who had discarded his female attire) by one route, and Flora and her attendant by another. They foregathered before reaching the little thatched inn at Portree, where they met young MacLeod of Raasay. After a short rest the prince bade Flora an affectionate farewell. They never met again.

The chief of the Mackinnons was arrested for his complicity in the escape of Prince Charlie and taken to London where he was imprisoned for over a year. He could not look for much mercy as he had been 'out' in the Fifteen and Forty-five but, in consideration for his advanced age, he was liberated. The officer, conveying the news to him, reminded him of the debt of gratitude he owed the king, when he had forfeited his right to life and property. Mackinnon replied, 'Had I the King in my power as I am in his, I would return the compliment by sending him back to his own country.'

Years ago many tales regarding the Forty-five were floating about, the authenticity of which is probably doubtful. One of two such is as follows. On the retreat northward of the Highland army, two followers detached themselves and went in search of booty to carry homeward. Entering a wayside cottage, occupied by an old woman, they detected a web of cloth. They proceeded to cut a portion for each. The woman railed and stormed at them saying, 'You will pay for this at the day of judgement.' 'Ah well, my good woman, if the credit is so long, we will just take the whole.' And off they went with the proceeds of many days' hard labour.

Another, which is rather of a grim character, was as follows. A party of MacRaes, after the defeat at Culloden, were making their way homewards to Kintail. They came by the way of Glenmoriston, and were proceeding to Torghoil to rest for the night. A piper of the party remained behind in order to wrap his instrument in his plaid. He was startled to see one of Cumberland's troopers, making as if straight for the spot. He hastily hid himself in some brushwood. As the unsuspecting trooper was passing, the piper sprang at him, and despatched him with his dirk. He coveted the high boots worn by his fallen enemy, and tried to take them off. Off they would not come. He then severed the legs at the knees, wrapped the pipes and them in his plaid, and continued his way, in the wake of his companions. On reaching Torghoil, he received food and refreshment, and said he would go to the barn with the rest of the company. 'No, no,' said the maid who had served him, 'they declared that anyone disturbing them before morning would do so at the peril of his life. But I shall make you a bed in the byre.' They went out, and the piper said he would sleep in front of the brindled cow: 'the cow's breath will keep me warm.' As soon as the maid left, the piper set about his task of getting the boots clear. He did so at last, and went off in company of the others in the morning, leaving behind the gruesome limbs of the trooper. When the maid went to waken him, she was horrified to find the legs where she expected to find the piper. She ran screaming into the house, crying: 'The brindled cow has eaten the piper, all but the two feet.' The innkeeper went out, axe in hand, killed the cow, and buried her and the *Sassenach's* legs in the same grave.

14 FLORA MACDONALD: THE END OF THE STORY

It is sometimes said that the three days' pilotage of the prince was not a pre-eminently great event. But it has to be remembered that Flora MacDonald did more for the prince than all his friends could do, more indeed than all the troops he marshalled for battle. A life is sometimes compressed into a brief space of time, and it was so in this case. There are deeds that shine, reflecting immortal honour on the person who performs them. Flora MacDonald crowned herself with undying fame by her courage, fidelity, and self-sacrifice.

It soon transpired that Flora was the chief factor in the escape of the prince, and about ten days after she parted from him, she was arrested, and put on board HMS *Furnace*. General Campbell, who happened to be on board, treated her with great kindness. She was allowed to bid farewell to her mother at Armadale and to have a maid. She was handed over as a state prisoner to Dunstaffnage Castle. In the charge sheet, 'a very pretty rebel 24 years of age' transferred to the *Bridgewater* in Leith roads. She won the regard and admiration of the commodore, and he simply heaped kindness on her. On 28 December she was put on board the *Royal Sovereign* and removed to London, where she remained in honourable captivity till July 1747, when an Indemnity Act was passed and she was set free. The Prince of Wales visited her during her captivity and asked 'how she dared to assist a rebel against his father's throne'. She replied that she would have done the same for him had she found him in like distress. The prince was so struck with her reply, and the charm of her manner, that he proved her benefactor from that hour.

Interest in her case was aroused in London, and Lady Primrose especially applied herself to the process of lionising her, and a sum of £1,500 was soon put in her hands. No sooner was Flora liberated than she exercised her influence on behalf of fellow-supporters in the rebellion. She returned to Scotland, on her way spending some time with friends in Edinburgh. She wished to avoid publicity, and longed for the privacy of her Highland home; soon after she found her way to her mother's home in Armadale, where she was received with open arms. Later she visited Kingsburgh, where she learned that Allan, the eldest son of Mr Alexander MacDonald of Kingsburgh, had taken the farm of Flodigarry. After a little time her engagement to Allan was announced and her marriage took place in 1750. After that Flora and her husband lived in Flodigarry until Allan's father died, and he succeeded him, and he and his wife and children came to Kingsburgh in 1766. In 1773 she and her husband were visited by Dr Johnson and Boswell. The eminent writer and moralist was delighted with his entertainment. The conversation, manner, and elegance of Flora MacDonald impressed him. On his toilet table after he left, a slip of paper was found, with these words written on it, truly a graceful compliment from a great man: 'The name of Flora MacDonald will be mentioned in history, and if courage and fidelity be virtues, mentioned with honour.' This noble and graceful panegyric, like a diamond from a rock, was extracted from a man who might be called the 'prince of critics'.

Adverse circumstances in the Highlands, and the call from the colonies, had induced many Highlanders to emigrate, among whom were Allan MacDonald and his family. The name and fame of Flora MacDonald had preceded her, and she was welcomed in North Carolina with unbounded enthusiasm. She received a truly Highland welcome from her old neighbours and kinsfolk when she landed at Cross Creek from the *Balliol*. The strains of the pipes and martial airs of her native land greeted her approach to the capital of the Scottish settlement. Allan purchased a farm and named the place Killiegray. The portents of war had begun, and Killiegray was not long enjoyed. Allan MacDonald joined the Royal Highland Regiment, and his sons were also in the war. Allan was captured, and four years later he entreated her to return to Scotland. Through an American officer she received a passport to Charleston, and with her daughter she sailed for her native land in 1779. The ship was attacked by a French ship. During the fight, Flora displayed her usual courage, refusing to take shelter, helping and encouraging the sailors, and she had the satisfaction of witnessing a British victory. A fractured arm was the price she paid for her intrepidity.

The peace treaty was signed in 1783, and Flora's husband rejoined her in Scotland. They lived in Uist and Skye till she died in 1790. Her end came suddenly. She became ill at Penduin, her home, and the same evening she died. Skye deeply mourned her loss. The funeral was the largest ever seen in Skye. The funeral cortège came to a swollen stream, the bearers hesitating, when one in the procession called out, 'An e sin a' mhisneach a chleachd ise tha sibh ag guilan?' ('Is that the courage shown by her who you are carrying?') At these words the bearers plunged into the foaming torrent. The undaunted warm heart, the gentle voice, the sweet charming smile are stilled. But she left a memory and example which will blossom throughout the ages.

The Americans joined the mother country in paying a tribute to her memory in a practical way. The Flora MacDonald College, in North Carolina, with efficient staff under Dr Vardell, sends out yearly young girls, imbued with the spirit, and inspired by the example of courage, fidelity, and humanity shown by the namesake of their beautiful college.

The sculptured monument on the Castle Hill, Inverness, bears the following inscription on the front, matching in part the inscription upon the Flora MacDonald monument over her burial place at Kilmuir. It reads:

FLORA MACDONALD

Fhad 's a Dh'fhasas,
Flur air machair,
Mairidh Cliu na,
H-ainnir chaoimh.

As long as grows
Flower on machair,
The fame will remain
Of the gentle maiden.

The preserver of Prince Charles Edward Stewart
will be mentioned in history, and,
if courage and fidelity be virtues,
mentioned with honour.

On the other side is the following inscription:

Erected by the Town Council of Inverness,
by direction, and at the expense of the late
Captain J Henderson MacDonald
of Caskuben, Aberdeenshire,
and 78th Highlanders.

There is yet another memorial to Flora MacDonald in St Columba's church at Portree, in the shape of a stained window and a brass tablet. The

The 'Bealach', the road over the Trotternish Ridge between Staffin & Uig
(Skye Museum of Island Life, Kilmuir)

James Budge, smith at Kilmuir, 1920
(Skye Museum of Island Life, Kilmuir)

Mr and Mrs Mackay and John, of Duntulm
Staffin & Uig
(Skye Museum of Island Life, Kilmuir)

Building the croft house, c.1910
(Skye Museum of Island Life, Kilmuir)

Uig Bay, from the north-west c.1880
(Skye Museum of Island Life, Kilmuir)

'Waulking the cloth'. Kilmuir women shrinking the tweed at
the factory, 1939
(Skye Museum of Island Life, Kilmuir)

Earlish post office, c.1910
(Skye Museum of Island Life, Kilmuir)

subject of the window is 'Esther delivering her countrymen'. The first light shows Esther receiving the news of the king's edict; the centre light, her appeal to the king; that on the right, the king with Esther receiving Mordecai. In the ornamental lights above are figures of angels, the MacDonald arms, and the words from Esther 4:16, 'If I perish, I perish'. The words on the brass are as follows:

To the glory of God, and in memory of Flora MacDonald, daughter of Ranald the son of Angus MacDonald the younger, Milton, South Uist. She was born in 1722, and was married November 6th, 1750, at Flodigarry, Isle of Skye, to Allan VII in descent of the Kingsburgh MacDonalds, Captain 34th Royal Highland Emigrant Regiment, who served with distinction through the American War of Independence. She died March 5th, 1790, and was buried in Kilmuir, Isle of Skye. She effected the escape of Prince Charles Edward from South Uist, after the battle of Culloden in 1746, and in 1779, when returning from America on board a ship, attacked by a French privateer, encouraged the sailors to make a spirited and successful resistance, thus risking her life for both the Houses of Stuart and Hanover. This window was dedicated to the memory of Flora MacDonald, in the year of our Lord 1896 by one of her great grandchildren, Fanny Charlotte, widow of Lieutenant-Colonel R.E. Henry, and daughter of Captain James Murray MacDonald, grandson of Flora MacDonald.

15 KILMUIR

Kilmaluag comprises the crofter hamlets of Balmacquien, Solitote, Conista etc. The island of Trodda lies far out in the Minch. The crofters of these townships graze a number of cattle, so many each, on the island. There they remain for one or two years, when they are ferried back and sold. No one sees them when there, nor can each identify his own. It may happen that some have died. The cattle are sold in a body, and the proceeds divided according to the number each sent to the island.

The earlier parish church of Kilmuir was at Kilmaluaig, and not many years ago the ruin was well above ground. Kilmuir was divided into the three districts of Stenscholl, Kilmuir and Kilmaluaig; the latter being central to the other parts may explain the reason for that position.

Of Kilmuir (Cille Mhoire – the Church of St Mary) every vestige has gone and there is now no trace. It is said that Reilig Mhor Chlann

Domhuill, the burial place of the MacDonalds, occupies its site, and here lies one of the best known of all her clan, Flora MacDonald. The present church is situated on the bare moor and is exposed to 'all the airts the wind can blow'. It was built in 1810 and contains 700 sittings. The building material had been landed at Camusmore, and it is said that to save expense of cartage, its present site was selected. The parish school would probably be erected about the same time.

Flora MacDonald's monument, Kilmuir, Skye

The Flora MacDonald monument in the churchyard occupies a commanding position looking out over a glorious landscape, and is a conspicuous object visible far out at sea. It was erected on 9 November 1871. It is a handsome memorial, a solid monolith of Aberdeen granite, taking the shape of an Iona cross standing twenty-eight feet high, mounted on a pedestal, a massive slab of granite. It was subscribed for by the general public. Unfortunately, the first cross was blown down and broken into fragments by the fierce storm of December 1873. Its re-erection in 1880 necessitated the making of a new cross, also of Aberdeen granite, and this was sculptured in Inverness. It was made in one block and was landed on the strand of Uig Bay. From there it was hauled by horses along the road to Osmigarry, where the horses were unyoked and the remainder of the journey to the churchyard undertaken by many willing hands. Being much exposed to wild wintry storms it has been supported by a great stay of iron.

About ten years ago it was reported that the inscription tablet had loosened and fallen and required attention. This was attended to, the necessary funds being collected by a world-wide appeal made for that purpose. Then, in 1922, a fine new memorial marble tablet was attached to the memorial, bearing the following inscription:

FLORA MACONALD
Preserver of Prince Charles Edward Stuart
Her name
will be mentioned in history, and if courage and
fidelity be virtues, mentioned with honour.
Born at Milton, South Uist, 1722.
Died at Kingsburgh, Skye, 4th March, 1790.

It was unveiled by Miss Emily Livingstone, Flodigarry, a direct descendant of the heroine; Major Livingstone MacDonald, another direct descendant, with a large concourse of people from all parts, including the president of the Flora MacDonald College in Carolina, USA, were present to do honour to the memory of the famous heroine, revered at home and abroad. At the ceremony, I met an old friend who remembered speaking to two men who were present at the funeral.

Placed over the graves of the Bealach Martins are two late medieval sculptured stones which Aonghas na Gaoithe carried away from Iona five centuries ago.

The legend of the disappearing piper is not confined to the MacCrimmons. The entrance to Uaimh an Oir is at Borniskitaig. A piper MacArthur marched into the cave, with his pipes sounding to the air of:

Bidh na fir uchda 'nam fir fheachda;
Bidh na laoigh bheaga 'nan crodh daire;
Bidh na minn bheaga 'nan gobhair chreag,
Mu'n till mise, mu'n ruig mise,
Mu'n till mise o Uaimh an oir.

Babes at breast will be warriors;
Young calves will be cows;
Young kids will be full grown goats,
Ere I return, ere I reach,
Ere I return from the cave of gold.

There are several caves hereabouts which were taken advantage of by smugglers.

Loch Chaluim Chille (St Columba's Loch) was two miles long and half a mile broad. It stretched from Camusmore to near Totescore. After two previous attempts, 1715 and 1760, it was finally drained in 1824, after six years' labour, at a cost of £10,000. The ruins of a Columban chapel stand on what was once an island. It was the resort of flocks of wild geese in winter. James Clow, the miller at Camusmore, and a Totescore man, took a heavy toll of the number. James Clow would creep up to the end of the loch. If the geese were not there he waited till he heard a shot at the other end, followed soon by the geese. James Clow then got his innings. At each end this went on till finally the geese swerved off to other quarters to be back again next night.

Chess-piece from St Columba's Loch, Kilmuir

Loch Mialt in Staffin, years ago, was peopled by hundreds of wild ducks, so much so that the crofters, whose land bordered on the water, had to light fires at the edge to scare them. Not a dozen now frequent the loch. Like most birds in Skye, the duck has dwindled almost to extinction. Widgeon and teal are almost unknown. Some geese and wild swans still appear at times. Luxuriant crops of hay are secured each season from Loch Chaluim and it is amusing to hear people remark, 'drying the hay in the loch'.

On the coast of Mogstad there are many creeks and caves which were long the haunts of smugglers. I knew an old man who himself took part in this. He had many tales of outwitting the 'gaugers'. The smugglers came from Gairloch, with their cargo of *buideals* (kegs), and were paid in barley, oats and potatoes. When the gaugers were in evidence, the smugglers were signalled, and the cargo hastily put ashore, or transferred to small fishing boats, while the smack held on to the Mogstad shore to receive its return cargo. The gaugers would board the ship and search, while the kegs were hidden and at dark pack-saddled to their destinations. Once a larger than usual cargo was expected. It was arranged that three men, who were suspected, would repair to the local inn at which the customs officers put up, and begin to drink and talk. By and by, as the accommodation was limited, they got into touch with the officers, who were not averse to join in the talking and drinking. One of the men and the officers became helpless, and my informant and the other made their way back to find the whole cargo well on the road to the different localities. On another occasion the lugger was signalled, and in a cove quickly transferred the cargo to an ostensible fishing boat, while she held on her course. She was shouted at to lie to, while the officers were launching a boat. She made sail and kept on until sufficient time had elapsed to have the cargo disposed of. The officers felt they had been duped, and hurried back, but found no trace of the goods. Many such tales old Angus related to me. He was a man of remarkable strength and pawky humour, a real type of the old-time *bodach*.

16 UIG

Baile nan Cnoc (Township of Hillocks) does not belie its name, nor does sunny Beinn Sobhrag (Primrose Hill). South Cuil, or rather Cuil, as there is no north *cuil,* faces Idrigil on the opposite side of the bay. The King Edward Pier was erected in 1894 at a cost of £9,000, shared equally by the government and proprietor, Mr G.A. Baird. A violent storm, some years ago, battered the pier so much that the flooring settled at an uncomfortable angle, since remedied. The pier is 1,040 feet long, giving a depth of thirteen feet at low water. The memorial in memory of King Edward's visit in 1902 was erected by Mr Lumley, Mr G.A. Baird's representative.

Uig, lying in a hollow, surrounded by hills, makes a striking panorama, as viewed from above. On the north of the bay is the tall headland of

Rudha Idrigil, a striking promontory facing the opposite shore of Cuidreach. Near Idrigil Point is Uamh a' Choinnleir (Candlestick Cave), so called from the use of candles in exploring it, or from stalactites depending from the roof. The circle of the bay is studded with substantial houses, including Uig Lodge, now the property of Messrs Cowan, the Edinburgh firm of paper manufacturers; the hotel, as all others on the board's estate, is 'dry'. A much-needed want is houses in the several parts open to receive travellers. Walking tourists have to hire and get back to Portree, which gets all the benefit. Such houses, well kept, would certainly prove remunerative.

Marines landing at Uig, Isle of Skye

A terrible disaster overtook Uig and the country around in 1877. Cloudbursts and incessant rain caused the Rha and Conon rivers to overflow their banks to such an extent as to unite their waters. Both bridges were washed away. Uig Lodge was swept out of existence, and the caretaker drowned. The Conon swept away the greater part of the old graveyard, and the bay shore was strewn with the bones of the dead and battered coffins. A promising young missionary was overtaken by water at the Hinisdale River and drowned. A correspondent with more zeal than discretion gave a vividly descriptive account to the old *Highlander*. The publication gave rise to an action of damage on the part of the proprietor. The action succeeded, and the paper did not survive the blow.

The new cemetery is on a rising ground, west of the Conon. A beautiful memorial arch, erected to the memory of the fallen in the Great

War, ornaments the entrance. A curious round tower stands on an eminence below the hotel. The object in building it is obscure, though built but ninety years ago. It may have been but the whim of the military proprietor. Close to the tower stood the old inn, a low thatched building. It was tenanted by Mr Cameron, followed by Mr Urquhart, who moved to the new commodious premises, which he held till his death – a genial host, a man of many kind deeds, whose memory is held in affection by a wide circle. Near the road stands the John Martin Hospital. The founder belonged to the Marrishadder Martins. The choosing of the Uig site was keenly contested, as it was alleged the founder meant it for his native parish. From the roadside I looked down on the house in which old Angus related to me his smuggling tales, and recalled the merry twinkle of his eyes, and the short hearty laugh.

The rivers Rha and Conon enclose what is known as Glenconon. Formerly it comprised Cuil, Bein Choinnich, Talamh nan Tighean, Beinn a' Bhrathaid, and the Creiche. I prefer the old names to one designed to conceal the cruel injustice of the past, now partly redressed. There was a contented well-to-do community in these hamlets, but, like many other fertile glens, it was coveted for sheep, and the people were removed from their ancestral homes and scattered to the ends of the earth. A few received smallholdings elsewhere. Some emigrants sailed from Uig between 1838 and 1848, and many others booked passages at other centres. Two got holdings across the river in Shiadar, but if Coinneach Odhar's prophecy is true, there was little for them to be thankful for.

Siadar sin 's Siadar,
Cha do chinnich duine riamh ann,
'S ged is lionmhor do chnocan,
Leaghaidh do chuid mar am fiar ann.

Siadar there and Siadar,
No one ever prospered there,
Though your knolls are many,
Your possessions will melt as grass.

Muinntir na sughan (people of the sowens) has been applied to Shiader people. *Sughan* (sowens) is not much in evidence today, yet in the past it was a very substantial addition to the daily menu. The *pronn* (coarse meal) is steeped in water in a crock for several days. Then it is wrung, the juice or water falling into another dish, and allowed to settle, when most of the clear water is skimmed off. It is boiled for half-an-hour, when it has a consistency of porridge, and when it is called *cabhruich*. Taken with milk it forms a light delightful supper, or *cabhruich bruich le sughan amh* (cooked *cabhruich* with raw sowens), when milk is scarce. *Sughan* was often taken with porridge. Additional sowens are put in crock for next night's supper. This is not new to the older people, but it may be new to learn that *cabhruich* formed an important food in the South African War. Mafeking was closely besieged by the Boers. Relief was long in coming, and food supplies were nearly exhausted. A Scotsman in the garrison rose to the occasion. He collected all coarse meal of oats and other grain in the place, and produced sowans and *cabhruich* on a large scale, so that Baden Powell could sit tight till relief came.

The *clach-ard* (High Stone) of Uig had lain on its side for many years, but it has been recently re-erected. The object in putting up this and similar others is wrapt in the age-old mysteries of the past. It lies on the brow of the hill, south of the Uig Hotel. The Brahan seer prophesied: 'Olaidh am fitheach a shath bharr an lair air mullach Clach-art Uig.' ('The raven will drink its fill off the ground from the top of the High Stone of Uig.') Over the ridge north of Uig is Scudaburgh and Totescore. Part of the latter was called An t-Earbull (tail), and the occupants *gillean an Earbuill*. Many of the older generation will remember *na geoidh*. They were three old maids living in Totescore. All participated in any errand or journey. With heads uplifted they marched along the road in Indian file.

Besides the elopement of Donald Mogstad and Jessie of Balranald, there was one from Cuidrach which caused a flutter in the higher circles of Trotternish and of the church. Alexander MacLeod was a young divinity student, employed as tutor to the sons of Capt. Murdo MacLeod of Cuidrach. Alexander and Margaret, the daughter of Capt. MacLeod, were secret lovers. They knew well that the MacLeods would never sanction a marriage between Margaret and a penniless student. They therefore decided the matter for escape; they quietly eloped when all was quiet in the house. They probably crossed the Trotternish Hills by Bealach Uige, a detour which prevented observation from the Cuidrach side of the hills. From the *bealach*, it was a straight line to Staffin where, by previous arrangement, a willing crew ferried them across to Gairloch. From there, they continued their flight to Inverness and ultimately to Edinburgh, where they were married quickly and quietly.

When the flight was discovered, there was great excitement; as we say in our homely Gaelic, 'Chaidh an ceol air feadh na fidhle' ('the music became confused in the fiddle'). We may be sure that the sympathies were with the young couple and that the old captain would not be helped much as to the direction of their flight, even though these were runaways, but he was too late, as was the case with Donald Mogstad and Miss Jessie. There is a greater halo of romance about the latter which is kept alive in song and story. The divinity student was afterwards Rev. Alexander MacLeod of Lewis. It was said by the unsympathetic, perhaps with some justification, that the young student abused the trust and hospitality of his employer.

17 KINGSBURGH

Kingsburgh was tenanted up to seventy years ago by Donald MacLeod of Arnisdale, Glenelg. He was a man of unimpeachable integrity in his every walk of life. No man of his time in Skye was more respected and held in higher esteem – a Highland gentleman in every sense of the term. His wise counsel in difficulties was often sought. His less fortunate fellow-beings found in him a warm friend, and often their stay in times of distress. The produce of farm and garden was freely distributed. Mr MacLeod was an elder in the parish church. He removed to the farm of Coulmore, Ross. At the displenishing sale, there was hardly a farmer in Skye but was present, and prices of stock ruled remarkably high. Of Mr MacLeod's two sons, Duncan was a captain in the army, and William tenanted the farm of Scorrybreac. Who filled the blank between Allan MacDonald VII of Kingsburgh, the husband of Flora MacDonald, and Mr MacLeod, I have no data to show. As well as Prince Charlie, James V visited Kingsburgh and the hospitality in Mr MacLeod's time was not surpassed in the former age. Creag nam Meann by the roadside would suggest there had been goats here. Tobar a' Phrionnsa (Prince's Well) is near here. The *crannag* below Kingsburgh is a natural pier, at which wool and other farm produce was shipped. The farm extends to the watershed and includes Sgurr a' Mhadaidh and the Baca Ruadh, a long narrow ridge stretching out to the *sgurr*.

Tha coire shuas-ad cho math 'sa chualas,
Bho 'n Bhaca Ruadh gus an ruig e 'n Cron.

There's a corrie up by as good as heard of,
From Brown Ridge unto the Cron.

These are two lines of a poem composed by a resident of Cuidreach, over a century ago, in praise of Coire Iomhair. Coire Bheinn is a fertile sloping hillside on the north of the farm. On the western and southern sides there are large areas of fertile arable land, including Gleann Aluinn Romasdail, one of the four best pasture grounds for the *glas gobhar nam Fionn*, the grey goat of the Fingalians. The river Hinisdale marches Kingsburgh and Cuidreach, the lower stretch of which was, and is, a famous fishing stream, of which the writer has many lively memories. Craigill at the summit of the glen was said to have been haunted by a ghost, who appeared to come from the river and float around the Craigill.

Kingsburgh

At Cuidreach is a curious relic of a former age. It is a square fortalice, built with neither door nor window. The building could be entered only by a ladder, and seems as uncompleted, though now only a ruin. It is called Caisteal Uisdein. All accounts handed down to us about this Uisdean (Hugh) make him out an inveterate plotter, dead to every virtue, treacherous to friend and foe alike, his hands steeped red in the blood of his fellows, insatiable in the lust of his depravity. His ruling passion was to attain the chiefship, held by his cousin, Donald Gorm. The latter little suspected, in helping Hugh in the building, that the keep was designed against himself, and all who might come between Hugh and the object of his desires. Donald Gorm, by stress of weather, made a forced landing in Mull. By an unfortunate chance, Hugh happened to be there. He 'lifted' some of MacLean's cattle. Donald Gorm and his crew were suspected, and he had to defend himself from the MacLeans, as a result of which he lost some of his followers. But Uisdean, in his career of crime, made a fatal mistake, which brought his criminal career to an end. He wrote a letter to Donald Gorm protesting his friendship and loyalty, and at the same time wrote to a William Martin soliciting his help against his chief. Martin's letter went to Donald Gorm and the latter's to Martin. Hugh was seized by local clansmen, and cast into the dungeon of Duntulm Castle, where he expiated his numerous crimes by a terrible death. There is a Creag Uisdein, and a Lon Uisdein in the vicinity.

The MacVicars were a considerable clan in North Uist at one time. They were almost exterminated by the ruthless Uisdean Mor Mac Ghilleasbuig Chleireach's slaughtering indiscriminately. The poetess of the MacVicars composed a lamentation for her brothers, and the other MacVicars that were slain, and invoked that some horrible calamity would befall him. Her curses got her desires in full measure. A stanza of the lament is as follows:

Uisdein 'ic Ghilleasbuig Chleireach,
He 'm bo ho lin lo,
Hu o hor ho eileadh,
He 'm bo ho lin lo.

Far an laigh thu slan nar eirich,
He 'm bo ho, etc.
Sgeul do bhais gu mnathan Shleite,
He 'm bo ho etc.

'S chugamsa me chuid fein dheth,
He 'm bo ho, etc.
'S do mhionach bhi 'n luib do leine,
Hi 'm bo ho, etc.

Hugh, son of Archibald Clerk,
He 'm bo ho etc.

He 'm bo ho etc.

Where you lie down healthy never rise,
He 'm bo ho etc.
Let news of your death reach the women of Sleat,
He 'm bo ho etc.

And let me have my share of it,
He 'm bo ho etc.
And may your entrails be in the fold of your shirt,
He 'm bo ho etc.

Cuidreach was occupied till about eighty years ago by a Mr John Stewart (Iain na Cuidreich). He went to India, made a fortune, and returned to Skye, where for a few months he resided, but not finding a suitable residence he latterly lived in Sussex. He was preceded by Major MacLeod, and his successor was Mr Alexander MacRae, followed by Mr Donald Clow, who afterwards occupied Kingsburgh. It is now occupied by Mrs Ferguson, a niece of Jessie of Balranald. In Cuidreach, near Uig Bay, there is the Camus Beag (Little Bay), near which there is a cave, in which the farmer's goats sheltered. An abnormal tide in 1872 flooded the cave, and the whole flock was drowned. A similar occurrence took place on the opposite side of Trotternish by the same tide. By the roadside in Cuidreach is Lochan nan Ceann (Loch of the Heads). Tradition has it that a number of bandits, on reiving expedition, were here trapped and slain, their heads being thrown into the loch. One of the many fights between the MacLeods and MacDonalds took place near here. An arch-enemy of the MacLeods lived at Cuidreach, one Donald MacIain 'ic Sheumais. In Cuidreach, near the outlet of the Hinisdale, is the ruin of Tigh an Duin, where Flora MacDonald died. Along the Hinisdale is a lovely glen, which is usually termed An Gleann, as pre-eminent among glens. There are here possibly some of the few economic holdings on the Kilmuir estate. Some of the holders on Glenuig, evicted many years ago, got crofts in the glen. The bridge was swept away by the flood of 1877, and has been twice re-built since. One of the evicted Glen Uig crofters was Ian MacPhadruig, followed by his son Peter. The late Captain Ronald MacDonald, solicitor and banker, Portree, who died of wounds received at the battle of Festubert, was a son of Peter, almost a centenarian, whose widow died recently.

18 SNIZORT

Borve was cleared of crofters about 1840 and was added to the farm of Skirinish. The tenant of my earliest recollection was Mr William MacDonald, a Eurasian, a man of outstanding presence, inheriting to a high degree the dignified bearing and handsomeness of the Eurasian. His father, I believe, occupied the farm before him. An old Indian who was about the place, Cheko, was perhaps his personal servant. Poor Cheko died, and was laid to rest far from his own beloved land of sunshine and warmth under the cold leaden sky of Eilean a' Cheo. Dun-Sgirinnis is a prominent landmark on what is called Iochdar Sgrinnis. There are several smaller *duns*. There is greensward of considerable extent, including an extensive area of fertile arable land. Sgeir nan Cudaigean, on Rudha Sgirinnis, was the resort of boys and girls to fish for young saithe. In the sandy shore every variety of shell fish abounded, and was a welcome addition to the daily food; it is not now taken so much advantage of. On the opposite side of the loch, forming part of Sgirinnis is Beinn Achaidh nan Bard ('Eachan', but more probably 'Achadh'), whose height is prolonged till it joins Beinn a' Chearcuill on the Scorrybreac side of the watershed. The following tradition may supply the key: Achadh nam Bard was a field held by the bard Duncan MacRuaraidh from Sir James MacDonald. His successor was the famous Iain MacCodrum. These bards held poetical schools in Skye. The last of the occupants of Borve was Mairi nan Gobhar. The goats, like Mary's lamb, followed her about. When she had to go far afield she had to pen them. A school, built and endowed by one MacDiarmid, for Borve children, was disposed of, and the endowment transferred to Carbost School. The question may arise: 'Have the Borve children a right to the school and endowment?' There were no children in Borve when the transference was made, but there are now.

About the centre of Loch Snizort, there was a famous *cairidh* (weir), Cairidh Mhor Shniseart. The wall was nearly a quarter of a mile in length, and could be trod safely over all. At the bend there was a picket, to fish which was the exclusive privilege of the tacksman, the rest being free to all. Salmon and grilse were got, and sold at the salmon fishery at Portree, or privately. Occasionally great shoals of herring were driven up the loch, and often fifty to sixty crans were landed. But the old *cairidh*, in which seventy years ago I often splashed, is gone. It was broken down, and today not a trace of it seen, inevitable by progressive encroachments on sea and land by the privileged class. So also the stake nets on Eyre shore, where sea trout were nightly got.

The shepherd no longer carries his *breacan* (plaid) with its pocket for an ailing lamb. On the farm of Skirinish there were two famous shepherds, Iain MacAilein and Tearlach Ciobair. They raised the black-faced stock to such perfection that they carried all awards at the local shows. On a change of tenancy, old Tearlach retired and Iain MacAilein became manager of Glenuig farm. Here also, he improved the stock so much that he essayed to compete with his old stock. When the decision of the judges was announced, Iain had carried in all classes. Iain, hearing the result, said: 'Tha am prize anns a Bhein Mheadhnach fhathast, nam b'aithne dhaibh san a thoirt as.' ('The prize is still in Beinn Mheadhnach, if they knew how to bring it out.') Ian MacAilein and Tearlach had a famous breed of dogs and both knew how to train them. On more than one occasion, their dogs were bought at high prices by Australian ranchers and their progeny may possibly be found on the Queensland plains today.

The River Halten separates Skirinish from the crofter hamlets of Renetra and Keistle, the subject of an old song, 'A' bhanais a bha 'n Ciostal odhar'. All the *bodachs* of Renetra and Keistle were of the old *ceilidh* type. Each had a nickname. Of an old maid, who among several sisters remained unmarried, an old neighbour *bodach* spoke as: 'An nighean ud a chaidh a dholaidh air Donnchadh' ('Duncan's daughter who went to waste'). The Halten was, or is, a good fishing stream, and a smaller stream west of it also provided good fishing. Like all other rivers it is now preserved. The greater part of Skirinish now belongs to Duncan MacLeod of Skeabost, and is under crofters, with economic holdings. Mr MacLeod is an enthusiast in things Highland, especially Skye. His beneficence in this direction has been shown in various ways: in the establishment of a fund providing old Skye people the means of re-visiting the homes of their youth; and for the youth of Skye or of Skye parentage the sum of £10,000, to enable promising pupils to make use of their aspiration. Tote to the south is the property and residence of Col. Kenneth MacDonald, DSO, a most likeable gentleman and universally popular. Skirinish House and land is occupied by Mr Campbell, and Kingsburgh House has recently been acquired by Mrs Campbell, late of Kilmartin. The Halten and Ciosdal streams enclose the farm of Glenhalten, tipped with Beinn an Lochain, the resort and nesting place of teal duck.

19 A CURIOUS CAIRN

At the head of Loch Eyre there is a curious cairn, Carn Liath, Ceannsaleyre. It is some 40 feet high and 400 feet in circumference. Its origin is lost in the distant past. Often did I sit on the top musing what could be its origin, while rabbits darted in and out through its loose formation. A local builder some years ago was removing stones, and came upon what appeared to be a stone coffin. He ceased and replaced the stones. The coffin was formed by stone slabs. Tradition gives two accounts of its origin. The district was once occupied by a Herculean race of the Feinne, who subsisted on the flesh and milk of herds of deer, grazed on the surrounding hills; Beinn an Fhrith (Deer Forest Hill) is in the immediate vicinity. By the river's side, at the foot of the frith, is Mainnirean nam Fiadh, the ruins of which can still be traced. They consisted of unroofed enclosures of various sizes, into which the hinds were driven to be partly milked, the fawns completing the process. The latter were confined in the larger *mainnir*. The hinds did not thus stray far from their offspring. There is Coire nam Fiadh, a narrow pass on the watershed, near Sgurr a' Mhadriadh, through which the straying herds were driven back to the frith. On the hillside there is a deep hollow forming a natural corral, called Sloc an Fheidh, into which the stags were driven when required for food.

Suddenly the whole herd disappeared, and no trace of the *sealg* (game) could be found. The Feinne were thus driven to subsist on the huge shell-fish growing on the shore boulders, which they struck off with large stones. Parties in relays were sent to try and locate the *sealg*. At last a *sgairt* (loud cry) in the Coolins came from the farthest *fir-lorg* (trackers). The *sgairt* was repeated from hill to hill, until at last it was heard on Loch Eyre. On hearing the agreed-upon signal the Feinne left the shore, hastening to the locale. Each Fingalian carried the stones they were using, and flung them into a heap with such force that the sparks set fire to the hill opposite, which is called the Creag Loisgte. The two leaders struck theirs deep into the ground, where they can be seen today below the Kensaleyre manse.

Such is one origin of the cairn. The other tradition is as follows. The Skeabost river was the boundary between the MacDonald and MacLeod estates. The river not far from its mouth breaks into two streams, rejoins, and thus forms an island. Each clan claimed the island. As they could not agree, they fought for its possession. A fierce battle was fought near where the cairn stands. After a long and bloody fight, both sides were exhausted, and called a truce. It was then agreed that the disputed islands should be made into a burial place, common to both clans. The dead were heaped together, and the cairn built over them. These are the two versions related to me by a friend, now dead, who was full of these old *sgeulachdan* (tales). In the graveyard are the remains of a Columban chapel. If its size was co-equal with the number of worshippers, church attendance must have been at a discount.

In this, as in most of the old resting places of the dead, are seen those warrior sculptured stones, moss grown, yet still definable after centuries of exposure to the elemental ravages of time. There is in it a bowl-shaped stone, which, it is asserted, is never dry. Though often there, I found it thus. But with dry weather the evaporation, I should imagine, would shatter this belief. The stone appears to be a baptismal font, and such are found about all old Columban chapels, and were not removed.

There was another similar cairn, but smaller, in Uig, where the destroyed lodge stood.

At Borve, the road from Portree branches off to Dunvegan, and soon takes the traveller into the MacLeod country. It is difficult to understand why the road here was made over Druimuidhe instead of round it. The engineer must have been a servile devotee of General Wade. Observant of everything, the late Joseph Chamberlain remarked on this to the gentleman who drove him from Kilmuir to Portree. The first road was round the hill, and why the abandoned route was dropped in favour of the present, where travellers either way have to walk a long distance, is incomprehensible. The motor car has done away with handicap. Stretching out below is the wide expanse of the Mointeach Mor, which once supplied Portree with peat. Were it centrally drained, an easy operation, it ought still to meet the demand, or it could profitably be reclaimed into pasture land, instead of being an ungainly blot on the landscape of Skye. There is the old dam that in winter supplies the salmon fishery with ice, which is stored for seasonal use.

Here were the cattle markets of old held. As they were the only cattle markets in the north of Skye, thousands of head were stanced. Many thousands were sold and paid for at the close of the day. Most of the small inns had tents there, some coming long distances to secure a share. Driven by road, the cattle were ferried across Kylerhea *en route* for Falkirk (An Eaglais Bhreac), the great entrepot for the disposal of Highland cattle. The drovers of these old days were the Camerons of Lochaber, the MacPhersons of Arisaig, Carrachoille etc. One local drover bought and sold largely. He bought throughout the country, and if no satisfactory price was offered at Portree, he kept on to Falkirk. He was quite illiterate, but should he buy one hundred or more head, he could remember the price at which each animal was bought. At a Falkirk tryst he was robbed of a considerable sum of money. Owing to his rotundity he was styled 'Am Buideal' (bottle). He was a fair dealer, and would never take advantage. These markets are past, and Falkirk, noted for its cattle trysts, has disappeared from the geographical textbooks. Periodical auction sales have taken their place.

20 EYRE AND RENETRA

On the brae face of Eyre, above the Snizort manse, there is a building of the better class of houses of the past. Previously roofless, it is now occupied by a crofter. It was locally known as 'Tobhta (ruin) Miss Ann'. Miss Ann was a cousin of the Rev. Malcolm MacLeod, minister of Snizort till about 1832. She is said to have kept a flock of goats, and from the produce of these supported herself in comparative comfort. The tobhta was previously known as Eyre House. At Eyre House, Prince Charlie and MacDonald of Kingsburgh, probably also Flora MacDonald and Neil MacEachan, visited Miss Ann's father, Dr MacLeod, who was recuperating from wounds received at Culloden. As the travellers were in no hurry to reach Portree before dusk, they remained for a time under Dr MacLeod's roof and, no doubt, the distinguished visitors were regaled with Highland hospitality. After bidding the convalescent good speed, they continued their way to Portree, where they arrived in the deepening gloom of the evening.

Below Eyre House a small stream called Sloc-an-Tollair flows sluggishly. It was long believed to harbour ghosts, and several of the old *bodachs* affirmed that they had seen the apparition on different occasions, and heard its swishing sound as it rustled through the night air. Ghost or no ghost, its vicinity was shunned in the darkness.

Renetra is of similar design and dimensions as Eyre House, and is also now occupied by a crofter. It was occupied by a Mrs MacKinnon, a near relative of MacKinnon of Corry, and therefore kin of the chief. Her husband, Hector MacKinnon, of the Ceann Uachdarach MacKinnons, had died before the writer's time. There was a son and two daughters. Mrs MacKinnon was a queenly figure, even in her old age. Though in somewhat straitened circumstances, she had the dignity and bearing of a true aristocrat. Latterly she removed to Edinburgh, where she died.

Below Renetra House there is a deep, dark river pool, said to have been frequented by *each uisge*. A waterfall of ten or twelve feet falls into the pool which grilse and salmon cannot surmount, except when the river is in flood. An old man of my acquaintance used a hoop-net, fixed between the fall and rock, and the failing fish fell into old Donald's net.

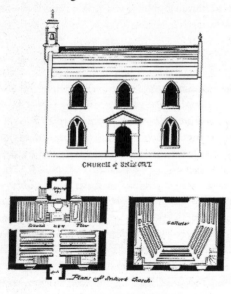

CHURCH of SNIZORT

Plans of Snizort Church.

Snizort Church

21 SOUTH SNIZORT

There is nothing very striking about the natural features of this part of Skye. There are no outstanding heights. They are merely rounded ridges, separated by streams and inlets of the sea. The slopes of these ridges are green to the tops, and inland is a wide moorland covered with heather. Yet these have a beauty of their own. There is the sloping green sward, interspersed with patches of purpled heather, the streams dashing between and here and there forming miniature cascades, quite refreshing to the onlooker. There are no towering hills nor rock precipices as in East Trotternish and further west.

The tides in the different lochs recede a considerable distance, and the land slopes gently upwards. There are many beauty spots. Caroline Hill is an eminence amidst green fields on the brow south of Skeabost House, and Skeabost House and its surroundings is a pleasant prospect. The Snizort River was formerly the boundary of the MacLeod and MacDonald estates. The river has a long winding course. It rises in Loch Dubhagriach, winds downward through the moors to the low-lying fields of arable ground, and meanders till it passes Skeabost Bridge, where it separates into branches. These, uniting further on, form an island, which has been the countryside burying-place for many centuries. Caroline Hill is perhaps the highest summit for miles to the west. It is verdant to the summit. That, with its green slopes and glades, with the windings of the river, present as pleasing a landscape as one could wish, especially if the eye has been accustomed to precipitous grey rocks and moorland waste.

Caroline Hill House crests the summit of the hill. The last occupant of the house was Miss Jessie MacLeod. She was a sister of Coinneach Mor Ghesto, Kenneth MacLeod of Grishornish. A sister of Miss Jessie was the mother of Lauchlan MacDonald of Skeabost. This marriage forms one of the links connecting the Gesto MacLeods and the MacDonalds of Kingsburgh into descension from Flora MacDonald. It is likely that there is a connection between the name Caroline and Carolina, to which the great MacDonald migration wended, and from which many of these migrants returned to their native Skye. Many Skye officers fought in the War of American Independence, in Carolina, and the name may have been an import of frustrated hopes. A Captain MacDonald, who fought in this war, resided at Carolina Hill for several years, and to him it and possibly some of the surroundings may have belonged. Nothing now remains of the house but two bare walls. One cannot help shedding a tear over the decay of these ancient houses all over Skye, and elsewhere, which once resounded with life and laughter, and wherein dwelt all that was best and illustrious in our sea-girt isle.

The modern house of Skeabost stands at the head of Loch Snizort. The house and its surroundings, improved in every direction by the late Mr Lauchlan MacDonald, is a beautiful and imposing mansion.

22 TREASLAN AND TIGH-AN-LOIN

Treaslan was the residence of John Martin of East Trotternish of the Marishadder Martins, who founded the John Martin Hospital at Uig. The founder meant it for his native parish, but influences were brought to bear, with the result that it was erected as said. John Martin was abroad for many years. On his return he resided there with his two sisters and a brother-in-law, Roderick Matheson (Ruairidh Muillear). This Roderick was the returning officer at the first School Board election of Snizort. He was buried in Culnacnoc graveyard. A relative of John Martin, William Martin, built and owned the Staffin Inn ('An Tigh Ban'), the first slated house in East Trotternish. There were many Martins then in East Trotternish. There are few now. The name is common in Prince Edward Island, Nova Scotia etc. On the death of Mr Martin and his sisters, Treaslan became the property of the late Alexander MacDonald, Portree, and from him to a nephew. The house is, like Caroline House, in ruins.

It is fitting to close with a mention of Mr Alexander MacDonald. He was factor for the greater part of Skye. During the land agitation he was subjected to much abuse by a section of the people, yet his heart was with them. Though they abused, they trusted him, and this was conspicuously shown at a school board election, during the land troubles, in this, the cradle of the agitation. Mr MacDonald headed the poll with more votes than the combined aggregate of the others. Those who knew him best, knew with what poignancy he regarded the increased rents on the crofters, foreseeing it would lead to disaster to laird and tenant, as it did. As factor he had to take steps that were repugnant to him. But many cruel and irritating actions were perpetrated without his knowledge. He was a true son of Skye, and loved the land and its people. He was not loath to miscall them at times, but another dared not to do so in his presence. He was always advocating and carrying out projects, benefiting land and people. The initiative of the new road through Trotternish was his. For many years the writer co-operated with him in this. Mr MacDonald died before fruition of the pressure, and it fell to the writer to receive from Captain Sinclair (Lord Pentland), Secretary for Scotland, intimation of a construction grant. Among many incidents showing his bias towards the people is the following.

A sale of household effects was advertised. The auctioneer failed to attend. A prominent land agitator took his place. He was cited before the sheriff. On his way he called on me for advice, which was to go to Mr MacDonald and frankly state his case. 'Oh,' he said, 'to put me down utterly.' He followed his own bent. When the prosecution case looked bad for the man, Mr MacDonald got up, tore the case to shreds, and the culprit got off with a paltry fine of five shillings!

Tigh-an-Loin (Burn House) presents the same features as Treaslan, but on a larger scale. The *lon* or burn meanders from the inland peaty moor, between slopes of fertile agricultural and pasture land, and enters the sea below the old Tayinloan Inn. In all these lochs and inlets, the sea recedes for a considerable distance, leaving large bare tracts of white sand, in which shellfish of many kinds abound. At one time fixed or stake nets were laid at low water, and these intercepted the returning sea-trout. The herring fishers of Loch Snizort used to visit Tayinloan after shooting their nets. The herring fishing has declined. The present generation do not seem to be so keen on fishing as their forbears, who were seldom ashore, when the weather and other circumstances permitted. In two of these lochs, the water recedes so rapidly that it is not an unusual occurrence to find grilse and salmon stranded, to be had for the lifting.

23 LYNDALE

Lyndale at present belongs to Lord Napier of Magdala. It is one of the beauty spots of Skye. The previous owner was the late Alexander MacDonald. Large fertile fields interspersed with green pastures, enclosed by stone dykes, are a feature of this attractive estate. The green fields stretch back beyond the enclosed fields to the inland moor, itself patched with green. Around the mansion house, there are belts of stately trees. The plantation was begun over a hundred years ago by Alexander MacDonald of Balranald. Planting began about the same time in several places: Dunvegan, Greshornish, Orbost, Skeabost. The Lyndale trees are very large. Oak, ash, plane, birch and beech seem to have thrived well. In Lower Trotternish there are only two woods at Kingsburgh and Uig, the latter a comparatively recent plantation. There are many tracts of land as suitable for planting as those named, which would supply employment in several directions and in time would be a valuable asset to the country. The late Lt-Col. Martin was for years advocating planting as a solution of keeping people on the land.

A later Mr Alexander MacDonald left his home in Lyndale to seek, like many others, work in the south. Though he began on the lowest rung of the ladder, he was determined to succeed. He rose to be manager in a succession of several large undertakings. From that he himself took work in hand, till he became one of the largest contractors in Scotland. The Wick breakwater was one of his undertakings. As the place was exposed, he took the precaution of having each day's work measured and recorded by the engineers. Thus any damage by the sea did not fall on him. Bridges in various parts of Scotland were built by him. One large bridge over a broad river was contracted by him. He finished it months ahead of contract time, and placed a toll on it, and levied rates on the traffic up to his contract time. The West Highland Railway received his guiding hand. The extension of the Highland Railway from Strome to Kyle of Lochalsh, a most difficult piece of work, was carried out by him. A cutting went through the solid rock, to a depth that no other similar cutting on a railway equals. Creag Dallaig of the Attadale Rocks was cut through by the indomitable Skyeman. The old people who worked for the MacDonalds spoke highly of the treatment and consideration they had for their workmen. Every Skyeman who wanted work was employed.

Mrs MacPherson, the Skye poetess, thus refers to Mr MacDonald:

Is iomadh iad tha seinn do chliu,
Le durachd mar a b' fhiach dhaibh,
'S ann chuir thu onair air do dhuthaich,
H-uile taobh na thriall thu;
Ni creagan Atadail a dhearbhadh,
Nach teid d' ainm air dhiochuimhn,
Fhad 's bhios tonnan uaine a' chuain,
Dol sios as suas mu Liandial.

Many are who sing your praise,
With good will as they ought to.
You have brought honour to your district,
Everywhere you went.
The rocks of Atterdale prove
That your name will not be forgotten,
As long as the green ocean waves,
Ebb and flow at Lyndale.

Some unfortunate undertaking by one of his sons led to his disposing of Lyndale to Lord Napier of Magdala. The densely-populated Edinbane extends for about a mile along the roadside, a memorial of Coinneach Mor's care and foresight. Across the loch a fine view is obtained of Grishornish House, the residence of Mr Kenneth Robertson MacLeod. It is beautifully situated, overlooking the loch, and is surrounded by trees. To the observer it seems an ideal home. On the coast of Lyndale is Eilean Mor Liandal. It is not a large island, but the largest on that coast. Pleasant are the memories of nights spent under the stars on the island, and returning home with the evening and morning catch, leaving behind a blazing fire of dry tangle on the shingle.

II

NOTABLE TROTTERNISH FAMILIES

1 THE MOGSTAD MACDONALDS

Mogstad was a separate entity from Cnocowe from about1720, when the chief forsook his haunted castle of Duntulm, and took refuge and residence at Mogstad. There is a tradition that an infant son of the chief fell from a window of the castle, and was dashed to death on the rocks below. The enraged chief, with bitter hate in his heart, vented his rage on the unfortunate nurse. She was placed in a leaky boat, with no oars, and cast adrift in the stormy waters of the Minch. It is said, however, that she was rescued and hidden until the chief left the castle. The agonised shrieks of the terrified nurse haunted his daily and nightly hours. That, combined with the spectral ghost of Donald Gorm Mor, forced the departure to Mogstad of the chief, Sir Donald, fifth baronet. Here the family resided for some years after the Forty-five, when the family seat was removed to the palatial castle of Armadale.

Mogstad was then acquired by Major Alexander MacDonald, proprietor of Courthill, Lochcarron. Major MacDonald was the son of the Rev. Hugh MacDonald, minister of Portree, son of Hugh MacDonald of Glenmore, son of Sir James MacDonald, second baronet of Sleat. It is said that the Rev. Hugh had two other sons. One is said to have been killed in war, and the other went inland in America. After this change, both the Cnocowe and the Mogstad families were still related to the chief. Major MacDonald married his own cousin, Janet, second daughter of Major Alexander MacDonald of Cuidrach. Major MacDonald died on 19 November 1855, and his wife, Janet, in 1847.

There were issue of this marriage two sons, Alexander and Hugh, and two daughters, Alice and Elizabeth. Alexander, the eldest son, became insane, the result of an operation for deafness. Being harmless, he resided with his younger brother Hugh, who then inherited Mogstad. The daughter, Alice, became the wife of Dr Millar of Stornoway, with issue Johanna and Eliza, residing in Edinburgh (1932). Elizabeth married

Captain MacLeod of Borlin, without issue. Elizabeth died in 1872 and Alice in 1870. Mogstad is spelt variously, as Mogstad, Mugstad, and Monkstadt. The latter is the earliest form, and we may assume it was so named from the residence of monks in the monastery of the isle in St Columba's loch, now high and dry. There is an old saying: 'Cha do thuig thu a dhol a bhuain am Mogstad.' ('You did not understand what it was to reap in Mogstad.') Tackling a piece of work almost or entirely impossible of doing.

Hugh MacDonald, Uisdean Mhogstad, married Jessie, daughter of Donald MacDonald of Skeabost, with issue five sons, Alexander, John, Hugh, Donald (of whom later), and James, and six daughters, Jessie, Julia, Bosville, Eliza, Johanna and Margaret. The five sons and three daughters, Julia, Jessie, and Bosville, emigrated to Australia.

Alexander married with issue, and lived in New South Wales, where many of his descendants are found. John died twenty years ago, about 1909, and left no family. Hugh married Eleanor Crisp, with issue. Donald, the Skye Lochinvar, married Jessie MacDonald of Balranald, with issue, among others, Hugh. James died in 1928, unmarried aged eighty-five.

Jessie married John Crisp, with five sons: James, Hugh, John, Godfrey and Alexander. Alexander married with issue, and lived in Adelaide, South Australia. There were also three daughters, Bosville, Eleanor and Jessie. Bosville Crisp was unmarried and resided in Melbourne, Victoria.

Eleanor Crisp married her cousin, Hugh, son of Donald Mogstad and Jessie of Balranald, with issue two daughters. Mrs Hugh MacDonald resides in Sydney, New South Wales; she visited Skye in the summer of 1929, and went over the surroundings of the old home of her forbears, no doubt much changed in the course of the generations that have come and gone since they occupied it.

This lady was the daughter of Jessie, daughter of Hugh Mogstad, and her late husband was Hugh MacDonald, son of Donald Mogstad and Jessie of Balranald, whose romantic elopemnt was a cause celebre. Donald, son of Hugh, first of Mogstad, was enamoured of Jessie, daughter of MacDonald of Balranald in Uist, and she returned his affection. Balranald objected, and favoured the suit of a wealthy factor, a Mr Cooper. Jessie was at Rodel, Harris, the home of her uncle. On the night of 15 February 1850, Donald, with a crew of eight strong lusty fellows, crossed the Minch to Tarbert, Harris, and made their way to Rodel, where by some sign their presence would become known to the young lady. As no response was made to their knocking, the doors were forced and the lady was carried off. Arriving at Tarbert their boat was soon beyond pursuit. Donald MacDonald, author of the abduction, was tried before the High Court of Justiciary at Inverness on 14 August 1850, and was discharged not guilty. The young couple emigrated to Australia. Miss Jessie of Balranald, Mrs Donald MacDonald, died at Hartfield, near Melbourne, on 18 May 1896, about seventy-three years of age. Thus passed a charming personality to her rest in a land far distant from the Balranald of her childhood. Her romantic elopement gave birth to songs still enlivening the peat firesides in the long winter nights. The elopement, on account of the position of both families, made a great sensation at the time, and for many years it was recounted by the peat fires in Uist and Skye. The writer remembers having seen two of the band, and the last survivor is believed to have been Donald MacKinnon, who lived in Linicro, opposite Mogstad. It is not surprising that the episode found expression in song. A nephew and niece of Miss Jessie live in Skye.

Sin nuair thubhairt Maighstir Domhnull,
'Sheonaid na bi 'ga mo chaoidh,
Mun tig an ath di-Domhnuich,
Bidh sinn posd' ge boil le 'n cridh".

Failte dhuit, deagh shlainte leat,
Se 'n fhailte chuirinn as do dheidh,
Failte dhuit, deagh shlainte leat.

Gur ann timchioll an Rudha,
Bha mi dubhach as do dheidh
Gus an till thu fein a rithist,
Biodh gach slighe dhuit reidh.
Failte dhuit, etc.

That was when Mr Donald said,
'Jessie do not lament me.
Before the next Sunday comes,
We will be married despite them.'

Welcome to you, a health toast to you,
It is a welcome I would send to seek you.
Welcome to you etc.

It was rounding the headland
That I grieved for you.
Until your return again,
May the way be smooth for you.
Welcome to you etc.

These two verses of this song seem to indicate that the successful attempt was not the first attempt. Or it may have been that Donald 'spiered' the lassie and was refused, and then took forcible action.

'S ann an sud bha hurly harly,
Direadh agus tearnadh staidhir,
Briseadh ghlasan, sgoltadh dhorsan,
Thug sinn mach i, 's neo-ar-thaing.
Failte dhuit, etc.

Thainig mach am fidhleir crubach,
'S gunna dubailte 'na laimh
Labhair e am Beurla 's Gaidhlig,
'Who is there? Co sud a th' ann?'
Failte dhuit etc.

An sin thuirt Cooper ri Allie,
'Dean cabhag 's na dean moill',
Gheibh thu mil 's baile fearainn,
Faigh mo leannan 's i air chall!'
Failte dhuit, etc.

Dh' eirich Allie moch 'sa mhaduinn,
'S thug leis an t-each bu bhras ceum,
Nuair a rainig e an Tairbeart,
Bha 'n 'Eliza' mach fo bhreid!
Failte dhuit, etc.

Nuair a rainig sinn an Tairbeart,
Fhuair sinn soirbheas nach bu ghann,
Fhuair sinn sealladh air a' churaidh,
A rinn air Cooper an call.
Failte dhuit, etc.

It was there was the hurly harly,
Ascending and descending stairs,
Smashing locks and breaking doors.
We took her out willy nilly,
Welcome etc.

The lame fiddler came out,
With a double-barrelled gun in his hand,
He said in English and Gaelic,
'Who is there? Co sud a tha ann?'
Welcome etc.

Then Cooper said to Alick,
'Hurry and do not delay,
You will get a thousand and a farm,
Find my sweetheart who is lost!'
Welcome etc.

Alick got up early in the morning,
And took the swift steed,
But when he reached Tarbert,
The *Eliza* was out under sail!
Welcome etc.

When we reached Tarbert,
We had the great good fortune,
We sighted the hero,
Who caused Cooper's loss,
Welcome etc.

Bosville, daughter of Hugh MacDonald of Mogstad, married a Mr Ross, solicitor, with issue. She died when only twenty-six years of age, and her husband a year or two before her, leaving three orphans, Sybella, aged three, Hugh Peter MacDonald, aged five, and John George, aged seven. John George died about 1910, and left no family. Hugh Peter MacDonald is (1930) still living, and has three sons and two daughters and four granddaughters. Sybella, who married Frank Grey Smith, resides at 6 Marne Court, Marne Street, South Yarra. She is intensely interested in any account of the family, and of the old home in Eilean a' Cheo (Misty Isle).

Jessie Crisp, daughter of Jessie, daughter of Hugh of Mogstad, married Mr Percy G. Jennings, and has two daughters living. The family reside in Sandringham, Victoria. Grace MacDonald (Mrs Munro) is a granddaughter of Hugh Peter MacDonald, son of Hugh MacDonald of Mogstad. Mrs Munro resides in Bingara, New South Wales. In 1926, Mrs Munro and her son visited Skye, and were disappointed at not meeting any relatives. It is possible that there were none, as the Mogstad family were a separate entity. There are several members, outwith Skye, of the family. At any rate, there are numbers of MacDonalds all over Trotternish, of whom some may have been relatives or connections. But the modern genealogist lacks the repository of the old *seannachaidh*, who had at his finger-ends the genealogy of every family, not only in his own parish, but in contiguous parishes for untold generations. The oldest families are predominantly MacDonalds, though the trend of successive generations has brought an influx of other clans, 'broken' or otherwise. It can be said, without doubt, that there is no clan name more numerous in the Empire and America. And a peculiarity, as far as the writer's observations go, is that they are almost universally tall and dark-haired.

The last surviving member of Hugh MacDonald's family, with the exception of James, was Alexander. He lived in Mrs Munro's part of the colony, and several of his descendants occupy thereabout. Mr Norman Hugh MacDonald is a grandson of Hugh of Mogstad. He is a solicitor and stockbroker, and resides in Wingallo House, Angel Place, Sydney. Miss Bosville Crisp is a grand-daughter of Hugh, and resides at Prestwick, Polo Parade, Canfield, Melbourne. Mrs Edwin Darby, c/o Bank of New South Wales, Coolamon, New South Wales, is another grand-daughter of Hugh. Another great or grandson is Mr Kenneth MacDonald of Thurlagoona, Cunnamulla, Queensland.

Of the three daughters who remained in the homeland, Johanna and Eliza were unmarried, and resided at Helensburgh, Dunbartonshire. Margaret married Mr James Todd of Underwood, Lockerbie, Dumfries, with issue Jessie MacDonald Todd, Underwood, Penicuik, Midlothian; Andrew Todd, Dunedin, New Zealand; and Hugh MacDonald Todd. Andrew Todd married with issue, among others Bruce Todd. Hugh MacDonald Todd, London, married Margaret MacLeod, daughter of Inspector General William MacLeod, MD, CB, RN.

Hugh and his wife are buried in Cardross, Dumbarton, where also are Eliza and Johanna buried, and later Margaret Todd, who lived to be in her ninety-first year. Almost all the Cnocowe MacDonalds whom I have been able to trace have a Hugh, named after Hugh of Mogstad. The writer's daughter got her name from an uncle, Hugh, named after Hugh of Mogstad, and his late wife was a daughter of Flora, the youngest daughter of Ronald Roy of Cnocowe.

Such then is a brief account of one of the oldest families of Trotternish, whose memory and nobility of character are treasured still in the land where once they had their home – a home replete with hospitality and refinement.

2 THE MARTINS OF BEALACH

Although traditionally of an older Celtic race than the MacDonalds, the Martins hived off into a separate family, with a distinctive surname, in sixteenth to seventeenth century, as many others did. The Bealach Martins occupied the lands between Uig and the Bealach, west of Quiraing, hence the name. They were the stem. They were closely associated with military exploits of the country. Under the MacDonald banner, they had their share of the forays and *creachs*, and later in the wider fields of national and foreign strife. As the Martins thus fought under the MacDonald banner, the history of both is intertwined.

The historical progenitor of the Martins was a soldier and sailor of some capacity and position in the early years of Queen Elizabeth's reign. He was Aonghas na Gaoithe (Angus of the Storms). His reputed wife was Biurnaig, a Danish princess. His second wife was a sister of the MacDonald chief. He had a taste for writing poetry, which led him into misfortune. The chief, Donald Gorm, had married a MacLean. Angus hated the lady, who persistently solicited him to honour her with an ode. He at last complied with some most abusive lines in Gaelic, long preserved. Such insult rendered his residence in Skye unhealthy while the MacLean lady lived. The fragment preserved was as follows:

Gheall thu nach gabhadh tu fearg,
A chailleach dhearg-shuileach bhreachd-ruadh,
'S daor a cheannaich sinn an t-or,
'S mairg tha posda riut-sa buan.

You promised not to get enraged,
You red-eyed, pock-pitted, ruddy complexioned old wife,
We paid dearly for the gold (dowry),
Woe to him who is durably united to you in marriage.

The above shows that Angus regarded himself as a clansman of MacDonald, using the word 'we' for clansmen. His grandson, indeed, was the first commonly called Martin, or rather MacGhille Mhartain as it was at first.

The chief, in view of his relationship, and the status and capacity of Angus, bore him no hostility, and arranged that he should leave Skye. Aonghas, therefore, sailed for Antrim, with a force of a thousand Skyemen, well equipped to assist Sorley Buy (Somhairle Buidhe), who became earl of Antrim. Campaign losses were disastrous to his followers, and Angus himself fell sick. The earl asked if anything could cure him. 'Yes,' he replied, 'could I again see my Skyemen in full arms before me.' This was impossible, but Sorley dressed up a thousand Irish in their equipment, before the window of Angus' castle, and asked him to review them. Seeing the deception, Angus broke out in abusive verse, terminating in:

'Gall bhodaich o'n Bhalgnaich Shlignich
Chan Albannaich idir iad!'

'These are old men from shelly Bolganach [a place in Antrim].
They are no Highland Scots!'

This shows that Angus never regarded himself as Irish although a lieutenant of Sorley, marquis of Antrim, and supporting him in the conquest of Antrim. He afterwards returned to Skye, when his enemy, the MacLean woman, was dead. In passing Iona he landed and took away with him the sculptured stones, which mark the graves of the Bealach Martins in Kilmuir churchyard. Angus' first act on returning to Skye was another ode to the MacLean lady. His antipathy followed her even to the grave.

Leagaidh mi clach 'sa charn,
Ged nach robh mi ann m'a chur,
Air muin fearnan Nic 'illeathain,
Mallachd . . . muin air muin.

I will place a stone on the cairn,
Though not present when erected,
Over the body of the MacLean lady,
May curses . . . one after another.

Angus lived in an age (1548–1618) when choice of language was rough, and hardly repeatable to sensitive ears of the twentieth century.

It has been said that the Martins came from Ireland. This is not so. After the intercourse referred to, no doubt a body of them remained with Sorley Buy, thus forming a younger or cadet branch, acquiring estates there and holdings as late as 1860. In 1838, on the accession of James Ranald Martin X, afterwards Sir Ranald Martin, CB, FRS, he at once received an address from two hundred of the name resident in Antrim, including ministers, clergymen and persons of substance, acknowledging his succession, and assuring him of their attachment. The form Gille Mhartain remained on the burgess rolls of Inverness until in the sixteenth century it was shortened to Martin.

Angus had seven sons, and some of these may well have continued to serve the Antrim branch of the MacDonalds. The common arms borne by the Skye and Irish cadet branch prove their common descent. In Ireland, however, the Martins had additional the thistle, denoting their Scottish origin. From Angus, the direct line of the Martins descends in unbroken line to the present day. An early instance of the mention of Martins occurs in the plotting of Uisdean Mac Chilleasbuig Chleirich against his chief, when he solicits the help of William Martin, residing at the east side of Trotternish, and this, as noted elsewhere, led to his undoing and a horrible death. It does not appear that William Martin was implicated in any way. It shows, however, that he was a man of some consequence, when the arch-plotter turned to him for support.

It is related of a Martin of Bealach that he was enamoured of a daughter of Mac'ille Chaluim of Raasay. The island chief for some reason objected to his suit, and forbade his daughter to have any dealings with Martin. But the lovers were equal to the occasion. Martin from the Creag Mhor near

Portree swam to Raasay, where the lovers had their interview, while the duped chief watched the sea for suspicious crafts. Martin in the end succeeded in bringing home his bride with the parental blessing.

At Inverlochy the Martins followed Montrose under the clan Donald, and with equal consistency followed Dundee in the resistless sweep of the charge at Killiecrankie, forcing MacKay's force into the foaming Garry. One, whose brothers served on this field, was Martin Martin, who was factor for MacLeod and had studied medicine abroad. He wrote a description of the Western Isles, so valuable in information and details that Lord Napier's Committee got it reprinted for the use of the commission. It is a pity that Martin, whose brothers, sword in hand, swelled the ranks at Killiecrankie, should demean himself so far as to dedicate his book to Prince George of Denmark. And one greater than Martin, Sir Walter Scott, committed a like indiscretion with regard to another equally worthless George, and well earned the trouncing of Thackeray in his 'Four Georges'.

> William and Mary, George and Anne,
> Four such children had never a man,
> They turned their father out of the door
> And called their brother the son of a —.

Angus Martin V received a tack of Duntulm in addition to Bealach in 1699. In 1730 the chief removed to Mogstad. His son, Donald VI, received a new lease of Bealach and Duntulm from Sir Alexander, for whom he acted as factor, and chief adviser in 1745. He was sent to Cumberland's camp, to negotiate towards averting a threatened invasion of Skye by Hanoverian troops. This he successfully carried out.

Martin VII served in the 76th regiment, raised by the first Lord MacDonald for service in the American War. There they gave a good account of themselves. At the battle of St James Island, they were called on to attack the regular French troops, under Lafayette. Firing a last volley, they flung away their muskets, and with claymore and target, executed their traditional Highland charge once again. Their energy was rewarded in the rout of foes, themselves of untarnished valour and discipline. This promising regiment was disbanded at the close of the war, and the MacDonald tartan ceased to be displayed in the British army; not so however the clan. The roll of honour shows, out of an estimated total of

100,000 of all ages and both sexes, no less than 4,000 took their part with corresponding sacrifices.

Angus VII retired to Bealach on half pay, and died without issue, and was succeeded by his brother, Martin VIII of Duntulm and Bealach, factor for Lord MacDonald. He married Margaret, daughter of MacLeod of Raasay, and had two daughters, Isabel, who married Martin Martin of Tote, and Jane, who married Count Maurin, a general in Napoleon's army, whom she met as a prisoner in Cheltenham.

Donald IX was a minister in Kilmuir. He married a daughter of Norman MacDonald of Scalpay and Bernisdale. Of Norman MacDonald's sons, three became generals in the time of the Peninsular War, and one adjutant-general to the forces. On the death of the minister in 1838, James Ranald Martin X (afterwards Sir Ranald Martin, CB, FRS) succeeded to the headship of the Bealach family. He was a surgeon in the Indian army, and carried out great reforms for the health and comfort of the troops. He married Jane, the daughter of Colonel Paton, CB. Owing to ill-health, he had to return home. Another link with France was created, when Ranald Martin's cousin, Leila MacDonald, a great-granddaughter of Flora MacDonald, married Marshal Canrobert. Canrobert commanded the troops who went to the support of the British holding the heights of Inkermann, when the combined force of 14,000 defeated 50,000 Russians. Canrobert was a great admirer of the British soldiers. Witnessing the charge of the Light Brigade, he exclaimed, 'C'est magnifique mais ce n'est pas la guerre.' ('It is magnificent, but it is not war.')

Sir Ranald Martin had nine sons, of whom six served in the army. Donald, the eldest, died young; Simon Nicolson, the next, entered the Bengal civil service, and found himself at Lucknow on the outbreak of the Mutiny. He was responsible for victualling the garrison, which held the residency during the fateful four months of heroic defence, through which he was present with his wife and two boys, who died of privation. Simon Martin fought in the trenches and was wounded in a bayonet charge. After the relief, he served with the field columns as intelligence and supply officer, and received mention in despatches. Reverting to civilian duty, he served a long career as district magistrate.

James Ranald Martin served in the Bengal Artillery until he attained the rank of major, when, disliking India, he emigrated to Canada, and afterwards to New Zealand. He died at sea. John Paton Martin served in the Bengal Infantry during the Mutiny. But disliking military life, he joined the commissariat department. His son served in the Boer War in the Mounted Police. John Paton Martin attained the rank of major-general. Cunliffe Martin joined the 19th Hussars, subsequently transferring to the native cavalry, most of whom mutinied in 1857. During a portion of that year, Cunliffe Martin served with the 14th Hussars, and with twenty men captured a rebel battery of guns, and put them out of action, receiving a dangerous bullet wound. On one occasion a rebel bully rode out in front of the British ranks, and challenged all to meet him. Cunliffe at once spurred out, engaged and slew him in sight of the opposing forces. After a long period of military and political service in India, he served as ADC to his cousin, Sir Donald Stewart, during the Abyssinian Campaign. He was present at the assault on Magdala. In the Afghan War of 1878–80 he was engaged, taking part in Roberts' march, Kabul to Kandahar, the action of Kandahar, and subsequent pursuit, for which he received the CB.

Norman, the seventh son, served in the 19th Hussars, was transferred to the 7th Native Cavalry, which mutinied, and he was shot down. Angus served in the 97th Regiment, including the Mutiny. He retired into civil life, and died comparatively young. Martin, the recent head of the Bealach Martins, entered the Royal Engineers, and after over thirty years' service in peace and war, and adventurous experiences in five continents, retired to make his home in Ostaig, Skye. Of his four sons, three – all who were of age to do so – served in the Great War. The eldest, who (with another brother also) chose the Cameron Highlanders, perished in the advance on the Somme in 1916. In 1915 he earned the DSO at Loos, the youngest officer in the army to gain that distinction. With only four or five men he held up the German guard in a trench for a whole afternoon, for hours throwing bombs at close quarters, until the supply was exhausted, and then, after emptying his revolver, continued to fire with a rifle. Eventually support reached him, but his action alone checked a section of the enemy's advance, which, if successful, would have pierced the barely-held line. Next year a stray bullet ended a promising career, when, like his uncle and namesake, he was only nineteen.

Such is a very brief account of the Martins of Bealach, whose roots are in the far distant past, and whose achievement, down through the ages, in peace and war, sheds lustre on the rock from which they sprung. Their burial place is in Kilmuir.

In addition to the six sons Sir Ranald Martin sent to the army, he launched two nephews, fitting them out, and sending them to India. Andrew Munro was the son of a sister who married in the Highlands. He rose to major-general, and spent his life on the Indian frontier. The other nephew was Donald Martin Stewart, the son of a sister, who had married Captain Robert Stewart, a descendant of the Wolf of Badenoch. Donald Martin Stewart had a brilliant and largely a fighting career, rising to be commander-in-chief in India, and field-marshall; he was created a baronet, besides having the Grand Cross of the Bath, and minor orders of knighthood. He commanded a brigade in the Abyssinian expedition under Sir Robert Napier.

Besides Lord Napier's landed connection with Skye, there was the association with him of Donald Martin Stewart, afterwards field-marshall, who commanded a brigade in the Abyssinian War, resulting in the capture of Magdala. Donald Martin Stewart was a son of a sister of Sir Ronald Martin, tenth of Bealach. On his father's side, he was descended from the Wolf of Badenoch. Sir Donald Martin Stewart was commander-in-chief in India. Besides Sir Donald M. Stewart, Sir Ronald Martin launched another nephew, Andrew Munro, into the army, who rose to be major-general. The late Lt-Col. Martin Martin, of Ostaig, Sleat, was a son of Sir Ronald Martin.

3 THE MARTINS OF MARRISHADDER

The Martins of Marrishadder are a branch of the Martins of Bealach. The former followed the peaceful pursuits of life, while the latter mostly took to military life. The first, so far as the writer knows, of the Marrishadder Martins was Martin Martin, who had Marrishadder and Garafad. There is, however, evidence, traditional and otherwise, that there were Martins in the district further back. This Martin married Rachel, daughter of John MacDonald of Culnancnoc, of the MacDonalds of Sleat, Clann Uisdein. He had one son, John, who married Mary, daughter of Peter Nicolson, a grandson of Nicolson of Scorrybreac, by Abigail MacKenzie, daughter of MacKenzie of Applecross. By her he had a family of nine sons and three daughters. The daughters were Ann, Abigail and Margaret. The eldest son, Martin of Marrishadder and Duntulm, married Isabella, daughter of Martin Martin of Bealach and Margaret, daughter of John MacLeod of Raasay. Later he had the lands of Tote, Eyre, and Unakill, and, as stated, was the last of the class called tacksmen, or gentleman farmers.

They leased extensive holdings from the superior, farming a part and sub-letting the rest. The sub-tenants paid their rents partly by work, so many days in spring and harvest. Fifty-six years ago I last saw Martin Thote, as he was familiarly known, and no one looking at the fine old man but would be impressed with the thought of the Herculean strength of that body sixty years before. With some friends I had called; when we were leaving he remarked, 'A spur in the head is better than two on the heel' – a proverb I have neither heard before nor since.

He died at the age of ninety-three. The second and third sons, John and Peter, died unmarried in the West Indies. Dr Donald was for some time in Demerara. He married Mary, daughter of Olaus MacLeod of Bharkasaig, by Julia MacLeod, daughter of John MacLeod of Raasay. He had the property of Roshven in Moidart, and later farmed Mogstad. He had one son, Rev. Donald Martin of Stornoway and Oban, and three daughters, Julia, Mary Ann, and Flora Hastings.

Another son of John Martin, Alexander of Inversanda, married Jessie, daughter of MacLean of Salachan. He had one son, Alexander, who was a banker at Portree, and two daughters, Marjory, who married the Rev. R. Mackenzie, and Mary, who died unmarried. Dr Nicol was for many years in Demerara, and was a member of the college of electors, British Guiana. On his return from the West Indies, he bought the estates of Northern Glendale and Husabost, the latter from Sheriff Nicolson's father. He died unmarried. Dr Samuel was for many years resident in New Zealand. He took a prominent part in public affairs there, wrote an excellent history of New Zealand, was editor of a newspaper, and a member of the legislative council of New Zealand. He died unmarried at Berbice. As already mentioned, Lachlan Martin met a tragic death at Loch Corcusdal. The Rev. Angus Martin was the youngest of the family. He became minister of Snizort in 1844, and ministered there until he retired. He married Margaret, daughter of the Rev. Alexander Nicolson, Barra, by his wife Susan, daughter of Nicolson of Scorrybreac, who was married to Margaret, daughter of Norman MacDonald of Scalpay. Sir John MacDonald of the Scalpay MacDonalds, who was adjutant-general of the British Army in 1830, and Colonel Matthew MacAllister of Strathaird, were grand-uncles of Mrs Angus Martin. Another distinguished member of the Scalpay MacDonalds was Lord Kingsburgh. The Rev. Angus Martin had six sons and three daughters. Alexander died in Edinburgh, John and Martin died in India, Samuel went to Australia, and Donald to New Zealand. Of the daughters, Susan died in 1908; Mary and Margaret, who was married to a Mr Fraser, a banker, made their home alternately at Husabost and Edinburgh. Nicol, the youngest, succeeded to his uncle's estates of North Glendale and Husabost. He married Emily Pauline, elder daughter of MacLeod of MacLeod, 23rd chief of Dunvegan Castle, and has a son, Norman Magnus, and two daughters, Susan Emily, and Emily Caroline. Nicol Martin is a member and chairman of most of the local councils, and a member of the county council and education authority. With the hard work, and constant travelling by sea and land to attend meetings of these bodies, Mr Nicol Martin's work is no sinecure. He is ever ready to support his fellow Skyemen, and not afraid to speak when necessary. There was no more popular officer of the Loval Scouts than Captain Nicol Martin, who himself brought a contingent of over thirty recruits to that body. Abigail MacKenzie Martin, daughter of John of Marishadder, was married to John MacGregor, who went to Australia. One daughter, Mary, was married to Rev. Mr MacArthur, minister of Portree. Eliza, the other daughter, elected to remain with her sister, while the two sons accompanied their father. One of the sons, John, was a member of the government, and Duncan a successful businessman in Melbourne. On the death of Mr MacArthur, Mrs MacArthur, her sister Eliza, and Miss Martin of Tote went to join the rest of the family in Australia.

4 THE MACDONALDS OF ORD AND SLEAT

The history of the MacDonalds goes far back in the annals of the Highlands; they were long associated with the Clanranald family – MacMhicAilein – whose fortunes they followed with undeviating loyalty. They are of the Clann Eachuinn of Morvern, Slioch Eachuinn Bhuidhe. As a family who, from an early age, entered largely into the social life of Skye, and are still identified with its local interests, it is fitting to record the Ord family. At the time of the Forty-five, the representative head of the family was Charles MacEachan, who married Mary, daughter of Angus Macdonald of Dalilea. As holding lands in Arisaig from the superior, Clanranald, he led a force of 120 clansmen and joined Prince Charlie at Glenfinnan. After Culloden, he was outlawed, but subsequently pardoned. He, however, never recovered all his lands. Charles had two sons, John, a well-known priest, and Alexander, who was a surgeon in the Glengarry Fencibles. He was the first of the family to come to Skye where he was widely known as An Dotair Ruadh (the Red-haired Doctor) and also said to have been the first to adopt the surname MacDonald. He married Margaret, daughter of Ranald MacAlastair of Skirinish and Strathaird, by his wife Anne, daughter of MacDonald of Kingsburgh. He had issue of five sons and two daughters. The sons were John and Reginald, captains, and Alexander, lieutenant in the Glengarry Fencibles and later captain in the West Indian Regiment.

Charles married Anne, daughter of Neil Macleod of Gesto with issue of five sons and three daughters. He died in 1867. Of the sons (1) Alexander of Ord married Maria MacDonald of Keppoch with issue; (2) Lauchlan of Skeabost, of whom later, married Willamina, daughter of John MacKenzie of Barvas in Lewis, with issue of five sons and one daughter; (3) Dr Keith, noted in Highland musical circles, married a Miss Niblet, with issue; (4) Neil of Dunach in Argyll married a Miss Brown, with issue; (5) Charles married Anne Williamson, with issue. Of the daughters, Flora married Alexander Smith, author of *A Summer in Skye,* Isabella married John Robertson of Grisornish, and Margaret married Godfrey MacKinnon of the Ceann Uachrach MacKinnons.

Lauchlan MacDonald, son of Charles of Ord, succeeded Mr John Robertson at Skeabost. He at once set about ameliorating the lot of his people. He materially helped them by providing employment, in making roads, in improvements to the estate and his residence, which he transformed into a delightful and picturesque mansion. While other crofters were fighting for 'fair' rents in the law courts with lawyers on each side, Mr MacDonald solved the matter by asking his tenants to fix their own rents, which they did to their mutual satisfaction.

This estate had changed hands seven times since MacLeod of MacLeod sold it, until acquired by Mr MacDonald. Before his time, there were twenty-four crofters on Skeabost proper. From emigration and other causes, only seven then remained. They were so situated that no proper use could be made of the rest of the farm. They were removed to vacant holdings on another part of the estate, and new houses were built for them, free of cost. In addition, he gave each a half share of the joint sheep stock club. He gave compensation for improvements to houses and land to tenants renouncing their holdings, and frequently helped insolvent tenants to make good. For the cotters, he built houses with patches of land for potatoes, asking no rent. On several occasions, he supplied tenants with seed potatoes and oats. To the poor, he was a real friend in time of distress. He was approachable at all times to the humblest and, as he spoke their language, he heard, at first hand, their requests and complaints.

Mr MacDonald is buried at Tote. Mrs MacDonald survived him for several years. As has already been said, they had a family of five sons and one daughter: (1) Charles, who married a Miss Housey with issue; (2) Col. Kenneth L. MacDonald, DSO, of Tote, of whom later; (3) Somerled, who married Mary Lang, Inverness. Somerled is one of the best amateur pipers in Scotland and an authority on pipe music; (4) Lachlan died without issue; (5) Ronald, who married Anne MacPherson, Sunart, with issue. The daughter, Lizabel, married Sir Lewis Hay, bart, of Park, with issue.

Col. Kenneth recruited the Skye contingent of the Loval Scouts and served with distinction in the South African war. He commanded the Scouts in Macedonia and the Dardanelles. To deceive the enemy during the re-embarkation, under cover of night, a small party of Scouts were posted in firing positions, and they were the last to embark.

Col. MacDonald takes a great interest in the survivors of the men who served under him. He is a genial and affable gentleman, widely and deservedly popular – as popular and considerate a landlord as was his father. He married (with issue of a son and two daughters) Margaret, daughter of William Caldwell, a Cambridge don, who had Morar Lodge for many years.

5 THE MACDONALDS OF CNOCOWE

Cnocowe, between Loch Chaluim Chille and the sea, was tenanted for many generations by MacDonalds, nearly related to the neighbouring MacDonalds of Mogstad. The genesis of the family was the following. Sir James MacDonald, chief of the clan, was married to Mary MacLeod, sister of Iaim Breac MacLeod of Dunvegan. This was a second marriage. They had an only son, John. With the consent of his eldest lawful son, Donald, Sir James gave to John a wadset of Mogstad, Cnocowe, and other lands, dated 27 June 1698. This followed on the marriage contract of John and Alice Mackenzie dated 13 June 1698. Apart from this wadset, the great majority occupying these lands were MacDonalds. John would occupy practically as chief of the sept, subservient to the paramount chief, his father, governing and administering justice and collecting his rents. In about 1720, when the chief fled from the haunted castle of Duntulm, and took up his residence at Mogstad, it is said that the family of John then moved across the ridge to Cnocowe, to make room for the chief, and settled permanently there.

The head of the family in 1745 was Donald Ruadh (Roy) who succeeded his father, Aonghas Ruadh. The heads of this family were men of consequence in these days and were consulted in matters affecting the clan. Donald Ruadh, scorning the attitude of his chief to the Forty-five, with friends of a similar frame of mind, buckled claymore and targe, and followed in the wake of the army of Prince Charlie over the mountains to Corryaraig, taking part in all the adventures of the Stuart prince. The chief would have turned a blind eye on the adventurers, an adventure he himself would have joined had the outcome looked more propitious. Be that as it may, the island chiefs took all possible precautions to meet eventualities.

Donald Roy returned from the campaign, and in due time was succeeded by his son, Ronald Ruadh. He was the last occupier and seems to have been a man of importance in his time. Raonull had a family of twenty-one, most of whom emigrated to Prince Edward Island and Cape Breton.

The fighting spirit of the clan is not dead. A great grandson of Ronald Ruadh was the first man to enlist in the Prince Edward contingent of Canadians for overseas fighting. Many have settled in the United States and further afield, as the years rolled on. These exiles are more intensive in their love of the land of their forbears and pride in their descent from the clan to which they belong than those at home.

From the lone sheiling of the Misty Island,
Mountains divide us and a waste of seas,
But still the blood is strong, the heart is Highland,
And we in dreams behold the Hebrides.

Of those who remained in the homeland were four sons and four daughters. Angus, the eldest and head of the family, resided at Uig. Aonghas Mor Mac Raonuill Ruaidh was a remarkable man, of huge stature, and Herculean strength. He married Mary Morrison, herself of abnormal stature. At Uig, from where his relatives and others embarked for the new country, he spent his long life. (One of the booked emigrants was averse to leaving the land which still contained his intimate friends and relatives. He disappeared, crossed the hills, and returned to his home when the dreaded ship was well on its way across the Atlantic.) Angus had a family of three sons and one daughter. The sons were all termed Mor (big). Hugh, the eldest, succeeded his father as the next head of the family, also settled in Uig, as did a brother and sister, both married with issue. The family is still represented in Uig. The third son, Ronald, went to Australia.

Hugh MacDonald was one of the finest looking men in Trotternish. He was the life-long steamboat agent at Uig. Like his father, he possessed all the characteristics of the clan. A scowl or the flash of his eye immediately cowed wranglers on the pier. He is succeeded by his son George, the present head of the family.

Angus had the combative instincts of the clan highly developed, and had he lived in 1745, Prince Charlie would have had a very desirable recruit. The incident with the drover I now give in full. There was a degree of urbanity, gentlemanliness, about him not discernible in the plebian stock of his day. Up to 1870, cattle, bought at the Uist markets, were brought to Uig Bay in smacks. The cattle were flung overboard, and allowed to swim ashore. On a Saturday in the month of July, a Lochaber drover, by name Cameron, landed two smack loads of Uist cattle in Uig. Several of the beasts got into Aonghas Mor's corn. Angus impounded them, and demanded £5 as the price of their release. The drover rightly thought that this was excessive, but did not wish to have anything to do with the law or police. He appealed to Mr Urquhart, the local hotel-keeper, to use his influence to bring the claimant to reason. Mr Urquhart accordingly agreed to use his good offices to this end, and interviewed Angus, while the drover stood out of ear's range, and the following conversation took place:

Mr Urquhart: Are you not an unreasonable man, Angus? You will give a bad name to the country you belong to. That is an upright man, a ruling elder of the Free Church, a man that keeps meetings in his own house, and speaks on the Question.

Angus: So, so, is he one of these? Often is seen an utterly worthless person indulge in such groaning.

Mr Urquhart: Come, come, Angus, be reasonable.

Angus: Tell him if he goes up to your house and stands six bottles of whisky, and a dram to every person who is there when we go up, he will get his beasts.

The drover was only too pleased to accede. Arriving at the hotel, they found a goodly number present, who had gathered to learn the outcome of Angus' quarrel with the drover. On entering the hotel, after a glance at those present, Angus rang the bell, and ordered what made a 'decent' refreshment for all present, and in addition six bottles of whisky. Angus did not sit down, but took his glass standing. He pocketed one bottle, and, turning to those present, he said, 'You men can have the other five.' Turning to the drover he said, 'Come along now and you can have your beasts.' And he led the way out as dignified in bearing as MacConnel, the chief himself.

One day Angus accidentally met the old estate official whom he so bitterly hated. After some cutting remarks from either side, Angus' fighting instincts got the better of him. The other beat a hasty retreat, and Angus hurled after him, in a shaky voice: 'You won't be long alive, and on the day you are put under the sod, the earth never before received such a lump of dirt.' Angus lived to a patriarchal age. With memory unimpaired, he delighted to relate events of an age now long forgotten.

Another son, Raonull Og, was a merchant and farmer at Kensaleyre. On his death, Peter, his son, while retaining the farm, transferred the shop to Portree. On the death of her husband, Mrs MacDonald removed to Portree, where she lived in Beaumont Crescent. Her home there was the rendezvous of the Peninsular and Waterloo veterans when they went quarterly to Portree to draw their pensions and where they sumptuously fared at her patriotic board. She was of a Kilmuir family, her sister being Mrs MacRae, Bean Rona, who, as already has been mentioned, kept the lamp lighted for many years till the Rona lighthouse was built, when she received an admiralty pension of £40.

Donald, the third son, was unmarried, and lived at Portree. Alasdair was an officer in the army and for seven years held an important post in Gibraltar. He was as huge in stature as his brother Aonghas Mor. On retiring from the army, he took over the Lochcarron Hotel. He was married, with issue one son and three daughters. The son went abroad. Mary married Roderick MacDonald, with issue a large family of sons and daughters, who emigrated to Chicago. Martha, married to Mr MacKenzie, without issue. Lizzie, married to Mr Lachlan Ross of the Royal Hotel, Portree, with issue three sons and three daughters. Alasdair Ross died unmarried in Trinidad. Dr Charles died unmarried in Lanark, and George married, with issue three daughters. Jessie Mary married Mr Todd of Kingsburgh, with issue two sons, and secondly married Mr Tattersall of London. Leisla, married to Dr MacKenzie, Newcastle, died in

1930 without issue. Annie married an army officer, son of General Sarrail, with issue.

The four daughters of the Cnocowe family remaining in the homeland were Chirsty, married to Mr Gibson, Portree, without issue; Kate, married to John Campbell, without issue; Flora, Mrs Donald Lamont, with issue two sons and five daughters, and Margaret, who married James Budge, an accomplished fiddler. It was he who composed the *port-a-beul* 'Cidh an fhidheal' ('Let me have the fiddle, hand me the fiddle'), in her honour when he was paying court to her. Two stanzas indicate her position in the family:

'S toigh leam Bean Thobhtacha Dubha,
'S toigh leam piuthar Raghnail Oig,
'S toigh leam nighean Raghnail Ruaidh,
Piuthat ghuanach Raghnail Oig,
Nighean urra mhoir thu.
Nighean urra mhoir thu
Nighean urra mhoir thu
Agus ogha 'n duine choir

I love the lady of Tobhta Dubh (the MacDonald home),
I love the sister of young Ranald,
I love the daughter of Red Ranald,
The elegant sister of Ranald the Younger.
You are the daughter of an important man,
You are the daughter of an important man,
You are the daughter of an important man,
And the grandchild of the generous one.

For others of the Cnocowe family we must go abroad. In Prince Edward Island, there are many descendants of the Cnocowe MacDonalds. Those traceable are mostly freeholders or peasant proprietors. In many instances their descendants occupy the original homesteads which their forbears reclaimed from the virgin forests. Of those I have traced, Frank Major of Margate is one. His mother was Flora MacDonald, a great-grand-daughter of Raonull Ruadh of Cnocowe. He served four years in the war, and was in hospital some months. A furlough enabled him to get a glimpse of Scotland from Edinburgh, but not long enough to get to the

Misty Isle, the home of his forbears. His grandfather, Lachlan MacDonald, and Alexander his brother, grandsons of Raonull Ruadh, went direct from Skye, embarking at Uig, and settled at Ashton, six miles from Dundas. There was another brother, Alexander, called 'Cape Breton Sandy', to distinguish him from his brother in Ashton, as he had crossed from Cape Breton. Both they and their wives are buried near the Presbyterian church of Dundas. Of Lachlan's family, five are living, and of Alexander's three living (1929). They had several brothers and sisters. John L. MacDonald and a sister, great-grandchildren of Ronald Roy, are on the old homestead at St Peter's Bay. Lachlan and Alexander's homestead was, as stated, at Ashton, and from there they visited their relatives, the MacKenzies, at Bridgeton on the Sabbath when attending church, which these early settlers duly observed.

Ronald John or John Ronald MacKenzie was the original settler at Bridgeton, now Dundas. His descendants still occupy this homestead. This Ronald was married to Kate, daughter of Ronald Roy. Among other issue they had a daughter Flora, named after the sister Flora in the homeland, who in turn named her eldest daughter Kate. Mrs MacKenzie and her sister, Flora, corresponded for many years. Later, another member of the family corresponded with the late Hugh MacDonald, son of Angus Mor, son of Ronald Roy. The present occupant of Dundas homestead is Mr David A. MacKenzie. A Ronald MacKenzie of this family died in 1921, aged seventy-five. His widow, Mrs Martha MacKenzie, is (1931) living in Dundas centre. Another of the family, Flora MacDonald (Mrs Anderson), is at St Peter's Bay. She is a great-grand-daughter of Ronald Roy, a grand-daughter of the Lachlan MacDonald mentioned above. Of Flora MacKenzie, daughter of Ronald MacKenzie and Kate of Cnocowe, there is no trace, though distinctly remembered by two correspondents. She is, of course, long dead, and her identity hidden under her married name.

There were other conveyances of land by the Macdonald chiefs, beside those of Aird, Mogstad and Cnocowe. On 4 September 1686, 'Sasine of Balvicquien and Claith in the Barony of Troternis to James, the eldest son of the late John Og; 10th January, 1695, Sasine of Bornes Kitaig, etc., in the Troternis Barony to William from Sir James of Sleat.'

III

MINISTERIAL HISTORY

I KILMUIR FREE CHURCH.

One could hardly find a Highland parish with such a succession of eminent and popular ministers as Kilmuir. There have been but three Free Church (or United Free) ministers since the Disruption. The first was Mr Munro, who was called from Tobermory, twenty years after that event. Simple and unassuming, beneath a pale rugged exterior there lay a wealth of love for God and his fellow-creatures. He was indefatigable in his ministrations, early and late, and his people returned the wealth of love he gave them. The sayings of the godly Mr Munro (Maighsteir Munro Diadhaidh) are often quoted by present-day ministers. Mr Munro, mounted on his small brown pony, was a familiar sight to the people of two generations back. The pony had it much his own way. Trot or walk, he was never seen to use whip or switch on his mute friend. Simply he could not. He was called to the congregation of Strathy in Sutherland, where he laboured with unflagging zeal till he passed the bourne.

His successor, Rev. John S. MacPhail, belonged to an ecclesiastical family. Two brothers were doctors of divinity. Mr MacPhail was first settled in Sleat before he was translated to Kilmuir. He was a man of commanding presence, and of saintly character, of whom it could truly be said that he was loved and revered by all who knew him. He was essentially a man of peace, abhorred strife in any shape or form, averse to the sectarian bitterness then, and even now prevalent. Often in his quiet gentle manner he chided marriage parties putting themselves to the discomforts and expense of a long journey to Kilmuir, instead of availing themselves of the services of the Established Church minister at home. It surely must have been a unique occurrence to have seen the three brothers occupying the same pulpit at Uig, more than fifty years ago. Mr MacPhail of Pilrig preached the sermon from the text: 'I waited on the Lord.' What a world of meaning was extracted from these simple words! As the duties of such a wide parish were becoming too exacting for his advancing years,

Mr MacPhail, forty years ago, removed to Benbecula, thereafter to Nairn, where he laid down the cross he so faithfully bore during a long, strenuous, yet eminently serene life. 'Sic itur ad astra.'

Mr MacPhail was succeeded in 1888 by the present venerable minister of Kilmuir, whose call was signed by over a thousand. Mr MacDonald celebrated his jubilee as a minister in September 1928. A large concourse of not only his own congregation, but of the other bodies in the parish, assembled in the church, presided over by the Rev. Alex. Fraser, Aberdeen. Other ministers present were the Rev. Messrs MacKay, Plockton; MacLeod, Durinish; MacArthur, Snizort; MacKay, Portree; and Dr MacLeod, Edinburgh, secretary of the Highland Committee of the Church. After addresses from the chairman, and several others of the ministers present, including Dr MacPhail, Edinburgh, the presentation was made by Mr John Gillies, Sartle. This was a cheque for over £400. To Mrs MacDonald, Miss and Mr Iain MacDonald were given gold wristlet watches, presented respectively by Mrs Gillies, Miss Annie MacDonald and Mr D. MacKinnon. Mr MacDonald replied for himself and family, in a speech which showed his natural force not much abated.

An outdoor service

Besides his ordinary duties he interested himself in every phase of parish and county council business. Like Mr Grant and Mr MacPhail, he took great interest in the schools and education. He was a member of two school boards, and later a member of the education authority. He had been chaplain to the forces at home and abroad. In 1900, after the outbreak of the South African War, the 3rd Seaforth Highlanders were ordered to Cairo for garrison duty. They were recruited mostly from Lewis. A request for a chaplain who could preach to them in their native tongue was met by the appointment of Mr MacDonald. A detachment of the soldiers met him at the station and he was cordially welcomed. He found on arrival that the regiment were without Gaelic bibles. He communicated with Edinburgh and a consignment was sent on. Time passed and inquiries at the station elicited no response. At length an Egyptian official called on the chaplain and explained that a consignment of books had arrived some time before, but fearing seditious propagandism, detention was ordered as no one could read the language!

After explanations, the official humbly apologised, and the matter was thus ended. Mr MacDonald was very popular with the officers and men. When the decision of the House of Lords deprived him of church and manse, one of the officers of the regiment placed his own mansion house at his disposal. In 1903 he celebrated his semi-jubilee. A large gathering of the congregation and many outside friends met at the manse, presided over by Sir Bosville MacDonald. After a number of laudatory speeches from members of the congregation, Mr MacDonald was presented with a dog-cart, and a goodly wallet of treasury notes, contributed to by all denominations.

2 KILMUIR PARISH CHURCH

The Rev. Robert MacGregor was minister of Kilmuir at and before the Disruption of 1843. He died in 1846. His son Alexander was his colleague for a number of years previously and was his successor. Mr MacGregor is said to have had an extensive knowledge of agriculture, and his help, guidance and example may have contributed not a little to the prominence of Kilmuir as the granary of Skye. A daughter was married to the late Dr Matheson of Portree, whose mother was a daughter of Lachlan Martin of Bealach. Another daughter of Mr MacGregor was married to James Clow, a prominent man in his day. He was miller, joiner, farmer, and, next to the minister, was guide, philosopher, and friend to all and sundry. Amanuensis to love-lorn maidens, medical and legal advice were all in request and frankly given. There is a romantic tradition about his marriage. It is said that at the marriage of Dr Matheson, while the ceremony was being gone through, James Clow and the bride's sister stood beside or behind with the others, and by signs, whispering, and hand pressures took the same vows as the contracting parties, though, at that time, it was not known that there was any such feeling between them. James Clow was an uncle of the late Mr Donald Clow of Kingsburgh. One day Mr MacGregor, on his rounds, foregathered with a man who was innkeeper at Camusmore, who went by the nickname of the 'Laird'. The Rev. Robert in a jocular manner inquired, 'Carson a thug iad Laird ort?' ('Why did they name you Laird?') 'Direach far-ainm, a mhinisteir, mar a thug iad 'am ministeir' oirbh feinn,' came the Laird's quick retort. ('Just a nickname, minister, as they name you minister.')

The Rev. Alexander MacGregor, Alasdair Ruadh MacGregor, as stated, had acted as colleague and successor to his father for some years before his death. I knew an old neighbour woman, who died sixteen years ago, who was married by him in 1841, 'da bhliadhna roimh an Dealachadh' ('two years before the Disruption'), as she expressed it. Mr Alexander MacGregor was a brilliant scholar and a highly cultured gentleman. He was devotedly attached to his boyhood home in the Misty Isle. Though frequent calls came to the promising young minister, he declined. So strong, however, was the inducement to leave, strengthened by the majority of people having followed the leaders of the Free Church, that he accepted a call to Edinburgh. He soon left Edinburgh, and was translated to the West Church, Inverness. Mr MacGregor wrote a life of Flora MacDonald, which, in his proximity to many of the incidents narrated, and related from father to son, may be the most reliable of the many 'lives' written of the heroine. In the literary circles of Inverness he enjoyed a more congenial environment than in that of a country parish. For many years he charmed a wide circle with pithy and interesting articles, under his pen name 'Sgiathanach'. Mr R.R. MacGregor, late secretary to the board of agriculture, was a grandson.

The Rev. John MacIver became minister of Kilmuir about 1851, and continued to be till his death about 1869. Mr MacIver was extremely popular in the parish. His wife was a daughter of the famous Doctair Ban MacLeod, whose medical and surgical skill was in requisition all over the Western Isles. Mrs MacIver herself was no mean physician, which was a valuable asset to the parish at a time when there was no regular medical service. Mr MacIver was greatly interested in the young, and always carried a packet of sweets to scatter among the children. He was a man of Herculean build and of gigantic proportions, and the last man one would associate with the work of a Highland country parish. Yet he was often on his visits, his long silver-knobbed staff in his hand. On his visits he was frequently accompanied by Alasdair MacGiorman, carrying his coat and bag. No greater contrast could be imagined than the giant form of the minister, and the short squat figure of Alasdair. Mr MacIver usually travelled in a cart; other vehicles of these days were very slight. He laboured in the parish for eighteen years, much respected by the people, kindly and helpful to them in many ways. A cherished memory of him still lingers in Kilmuir. He died mourned by all. Mr MacIver's father was minister of Glenelg, and a brother minister of Sleat.

Mr MacKenzie was seven years in the parish when he accepted a call to Gigha, leaving a church with few adherents, and going to one where there were no Free Church people. Rev. James Grant, a native of Strathspey, succeeded to the vacant charge in 1878. As a preacher he was more practical then evangelical. He invoked a measure of criticism on the part of some of his hearers, as he did not spare transgressors. Mr Grant studied medicine for a time, but realising that an injured hand would hamper him in that profession, turned to the church. His medical knowledge was often in request, even outside his own parish, for man and beast. Many of Mr Grant's prescriptions are even yet held in high estimation. While holding his own church as pre-eminent, there was not a shadow of sectarianism about him. He was a distinguished educationist, and was successively chairman, clerk and member of two school boards, and for many years chairman of the parish council. He was also clerk of Presbytery. His death was deeply mourned by old and young. He was a real parish minister, making no distinction whom he visited, and universally welcomed at the homes. He died in 1906. There have been several incumbents since, but the charge is now (1929) vacant.

The Free Church, which, by the House of Lords decision, became invested in the church and manse, has a considerable following in Kilmuir, as also in the parliamentary parish of Stenscholl; it is ministered to by the Rev. Kenneth MacRae, whose office in attending both sides of the parish is no sinecure. It is notable that Mr MacRae is one of three ministers whose Gaelic was acquired; the others were Mr MacPhail and Mr MacKay. Both Mr MacPhail and Mr MacRae had a complete mastery of the language.

3 STENSCHOLL PARISH

About 1828 the parliamentary parish of Stenscholl was formed, by including, besides a part of Kilmuir, that part of the parish of Snizort lying east of the watershed. From then the minister of Snizort ceased his visits. There was now no occasion, as the people were removed. The first minister of the newly-created parish was the Rev. John Nicolson, who was inducted in 1829, and died in 1837, and was succeeded by Mr Beatson, who was minister at the Disruption. Mr Beatson was somewhat undecided in his aspect of that event, but ultimately remained in. He was subsequently translated to Barra. More than sixty years ago, I met the old man – amiable, kind, and hospitable to a degree; the wrinkled face lit up as he was questioned about his old parish. He died in Glasgow some years after, in the home of his daughter, who was married to Mr Donald, the lifelong purser of the *Dunara Castle*. After Mr Beatson, there were seven ministers in succession. The present incumbent is the Rev. Norman Laing, a native of Uist. Mr Laing is very popular, hospitable, and genial. He is very mindful of the poor, helping them materially in various ways.

The Free Presbyterians have a compact congregation, equal to the other congregations. At communion seasons they have from Mr Laing the use of his church. There are eight churches in the combined parish, surely a waste of energy and wealth. It is, however, promising to note more tolerance and the absence of the prejudice and bitterness of the past.

4 SNIZORT PARISH

The Rev. Malcolm MacLeod was minister of Snizort till his death in 1832. He was succeeded by a Mr MacLachlan, who had a short ministry. He in turn was succeeded by Rev. Roderick MacLeod, who was born in Snizort in 1795. The Rev. Malcolm told the following against himself. As he and his son Roderick, then in his early college days, were returning from church, the latter remarked to his father, 'Thug thu gu leor de bhrochan gun salann dhaibh an diugh.' ('You gave them a surfeit of porridge without salt today.') It shows that the young student had not much faith in the efficacy of his father's sermons. Roderick's natural force of character enabled him to maintain a position among his youthful compeers. He became an eminent student at college. He was licensed by the Presbytery of Skye, and inducted to the parish of Bracadale in 1854.

He married Annie MacDonald, daughter of Donald MacDonald of Skeabost, who pre-deceased him in 1837. He seceded in 1843. By his activities on behalf of the new church, he was soon recognised as the protagonist of the Disruption in Skye and the Isles. His labours at this time were toilsome, as he was sent on several missions to the Isles on behalf of the new church, and only unusual physical energy and enthusiasm for his work could have coped with the strain involved in this arduous undertaking. On account of his eminent services he was elected in 1863 moderator of the General Assembly. On the day he was to address the Assembly an acquaintance of the family met his sister, who said, 'B'aill leam gu'n robh mo theanga aig Ruaraidh mo bhrathair an diugh.' ('I wish Rory my brother had my tongue today.') Mr Ruaraidh was on most friendly terms with his successor in the parish church. They were youthful companions. He was a broad-minded man, utterly above the bitterness and extreme sectarianism in many quarters at this time. There is no name spoken of in Skye with more reverence and affection than that of Mr Ruaraidh. His uncommon natural gifts and his magnetic personality could not fail to attract affection and admiration. At his last communion service, he was assisted by the Rev. J.S. MacPhail, later of Kilmuir. Mr Ruaraidh was just able to set the service a-going, and took no further part in it. I have heard it remarked that Mr Ruaraidh's mantle fell on the Rev. John S. MacPhail, and it could not fall on anyone more worthy. The following is part of a lament by a highly-respected elder of Mr Ruaraidh's, the late Mr Archibald Gillies:

Tha sgir Shniseart an diugh fo bhron,
Chan ioghnadh, 's mor a chaill i.
Chaill i ceannard anns gach doigh,
Is lochran anns an oidhche.
Chaill i 'm buachaill' 'san robh iuil,
'S an t-ughdarras mar cheannard;
'S an h-uile ceum a rinn e falbh,
Tha dearbhadh air mo chainnt-sa.

Fhad 's a dh'fhan sinn ann ar tamh,
Ag eisdeach gair nan alltan;
An duthaich Bhabilon an sas,
Ar clarsaichean gun srann ac',

Air geugan seilich crochte suas.
Cha chluinnear fuaim 'nar campa,
Ach caoidh is bron na laigh fo'n fhoid,

Nach till na's mo d'ar n-ionnsaidh.
Sin ri caoidh na laigh 'san uaigh,
'S ann bhuainn tha 'n t-aobhar ionndrainn.
Maighstir Ruaraidh, ceann nam buadh;
Nuair rachadh suas do'n chubaid,
Bhiodh osna throm bho ghrunnd a chleibh,
Is staid a threud 'ga chiurradh,
'S e 'gam faicinn ann an sas,
Fo chumhachd bais gun dusgadh.

Ged a rinn sinn luaidh air t'ainm,
A thaobh do dhealbh 's do mhorachd,
Cha do dh'eirich ann ar la,
Na thogadh t'aite comhladh.
A thaobh do ghliocais is do rian,
Do Dhiadhachd agus t'eolais,
Bha thu 'na 'teiseamplair do'n treud.
'S na h-uile ceum cho comhnard,

Na lionas t'aite dhuinn cha d'fhuair,
'S cha dual dhuinn fad 's is beo sinn.
Bha thu baidheil ris a' chloinn,
'S 'na d' shaighdear far 'm bu choir dhuit.
'S an dream a cheangail riut le gradh,
'Na d' dheidh tha craiteach, bronach,
Ag caoidh an diugh nach robh thu ann,
Bho'n theann iad ris a' chomhstrith.

Tha thu nis 'na d' sholas lan,
Aig fois 'na d' aite-comhnuidh.
Do phailm 's do chlarsach 'na do laimh,
A' seinn gu binn an orain,
Do'n Ti rinn sagart dhiot is righ.
'S a dh'ionnlaid bhuait do neo-ghlain',

'S a shiab na deuraibh bho do shuil,
'S a chuir an crun le gloir ort.

Thig thu fathast anns na neulaibh,
'N comunn Dhe 's nan aiglibh,
Chum gach cuis a thoirt gu crich,
'S an Fhirinn, mar a gheall thu;
Mar chaidh E suas gu'n tig E nuas,
A ghairm a shluaigh gu cunntas:
Bidh Maighstir Ruaraidh cur Amen,
Ri sgrios a' mheud 's dhiult E.

The district of Snizort is today in sorrow,
Little wonder, great was her loss.
She lost a leader in every way,
And a lantern in the night.
She lost the herdsman who had guidance,
And authority as a leader;
And every step he made in his way,
Proves my words.

As long as we remained at ease,
Listening to the murmur of the brooks;
Enthralled in the country of Babylon,
Our harps silent,
Hanging up on willow branches.
No sound could be heard in our camps,
But lamenting and mourning him who lies beneath the sod,
And will, no more, return to us.

We mourn him lying in the grave,
And we have good reason to lament.
Mr Roderick, acme of talent;
When he ascended the pulpit,
A heavy sigh issued from the depth of his being.
Pained by the state of his flock,
And seeing them locked
In the power of eternal death.

Although we gloried in your name,
For your appearance and stature,
There did not arise in our day
One who could take your place with you.
Because of your wisdom and your sensibility,
Your godliness and knowledge.
You were an example to your flock.
So even in every step.

One who can fill your place for us is not found,
And unlikely to be during our lifetime.
You were gentle with the children,
And a soldier when required to be.
And those who stood by you in love,
Are pained and sorrowful after you,
Lamenting today that you are not there,
Since they have begun the dispute. *

You are now in your full joy,
At rest in your dwelling.
Your palm and harp in your hand,
Sweetly singing the hymn,
To the one who made you priest and king.
And washed from you your uncleanliness,
And wiped the tears from your eyes,
And put the crown of glory on you.

You will come again from the heavens,
In company with God and the angels,
To bring every thing to an end,
As you promised in scripture;
As He went up, so He will come down,
To call the multitude to account;
Mr Roderick will be putting Amen,
To the destruction to the many who refused him.

* The mutual eligibity troubles.

Open air service in Skye

The Rev. Angus Martin became minister of Snizort in 1844, in succession to the Rev. Roderick MacLeod. He was the youngest son of the last family of the Martins of Marrishadder. He was a courtly gentleman of the old school, and one of the foremost Gaelic preachers of his day. His friendship in early life with the Rev. Roderick MacLeod, though now in different denominations, remained unbroken until the death of the latter. He married Margaret, daughter of the Rev. Alexander Nicholson of Barra, by his wife Susan, only daughter of Donald Nicolson of Scorrybreac, who was married to Margaret, daughter of MacDonald of Scalpay. By this marriage, Sir John MacDonald of the MacDonalds of Scalpa, adjutant-general of the British Army in 1830, and Colonel Matthew MacAllister of Straithaird, were grand-uncles of Mrs Martin. Mr Martin's family, though in a different walk of life, occupied important positions. Three brothers were doctors, one was a member of the college of electors, British Guiana; another was a member of the legislative council of New Zealand, wrote a history of New Zealand, and was editor of a newspaper. Mrs Martin was a lady of exceptional charm of manner, universally revered in the wide circle in which she moved. Her death was a terrible shock, not only to Mr Martin and family, but to the whole parish. On the funeral day the Rev. Roderick MacLeod bore one end of the coffin out of the manse, and at the grave delivered an address, setting forth her inspiring example as a wife, mother and friend. Mr Martin's eldest daughter, Susan, equally revered, assumed the vacant place. Mr Martin continued his ministry till failing health compelled his retirement, and he resided afterwards with his son, Nicol of Glendale.

While Maighsteir Ruaraidh and Maighsteir Aonghas, as they were called, were the outstanding ministers at the time of the Disruption, several have occupied each church since.

The present minister of the Established Church is the Rev. Donald MacArthur, who is a native of Kilmuir. He was translated from the parish of Lochs, Lewis. The MacArthurs were numerous in Kilmuir, where they were hereditary pipers to the MacDonald chiefs. Mr MacArthur is in the prime of life, an accomplished preacher, with an earnest persuasive delivery that attracts attention. He is genial and hospitable, and is respected by all sections of the community. There is no sectarianism in Mr MacArthur, and the mellowing influence of recent years finds a responsive note in his official and ordinary conduct.

Mr Joseph Lamont succeeded Mr Ruaraidh. He was an able preacher. He was at a disadvantage in succeeding his pre-eminent predecessor. The mutual eligibility trouble arose, and Mr Lamont was subjected to much abuse, regretted keenly by friends and opponents. He was translated to Rosehall.

Mr MacDougall (now United Free), from Lochs parish in Lewis, followed Mr Lamont, retired, and died recently in Lochalsh. Both Mr Lamont and Mr MacDougall were in great request at communion services.

In the Free Church the Rev. Mr MacRury succeeded Mr Lamont. Mr MacRury was a man of cultured mind, and an eminent Gaelic scholar, and wrote several books in that language. He was not of robust constitution, and died after a few years of ministry.

The Rev. John Stewart succeeded. He was exceedingly mindful of the poor, making no distinction of what body they belonged to. His hobby was sailing, and he built his own boats. He even built a small yacht, in which alone he sailed to his new charge in Mull. Later he returned to Kilmuir for a short ministry. His sailing hobby recalls another minister with similar tastes, who said of himself, 'Is mairg a mhill deagh sheoladair le droch mhinisteir.' ('A pity to spoil a good sailor by a bad minister.') The Rev. Mr MacKay, after some years of ministry, removed to Clyne, and was succeeded by the present incumbent, Mr MacKenzie, who came to the parish with high credentials from his former charge.

5 CLERGY AND LAY PREACHERS OF THE PAST

Some of the present-day and past ministers, and more especially lay missionaries, tabooed the fiddle, bagpipes, and every *inneal ciuil* (musical instrument). One of the most famous and respected missionaries in Trotternish, Raonull Mac Phadruig, was an exception. Ronald was returning from his weekend service at Snizort, when he was joined on the way by a piper from Kilmuir. The day was warm, and they rested beside a spring. Ronald requested the piper to take out his pipes and play. The piper was taken aback at the request, and remarked that he thought he would be against such. 'No, I am not, and more especially if you make an honest living by it,' said Ronald. The piper played several tunes as they sat by the spring. Ronald thanked the piper, saying he liked the sound of the pipes.

There was a testy old missionary layman, who on his rounds put up at a certain house, where he would be requested to conduct family worship. He was peculiar in manner, as well as in speech. In the house there were several young sons. While the service proceeded, the risible feelings of the boys could not be suppressed, and found expression in mumbled tittering. The missionary turned angrily and said, 'Tha an diabhul 'na bhur measg, 'illean.' ('The devil is among you, boys.') For a time there was 'silence deep as death'. But the boys' feelings could not be controlled, and a renewal of the tittering roused his wrath anew, and he said, with some emphasis: 'Tha e fhathast ann.' ('He is still there.')

A minister was called upon by a woman who asked him to go to see one of her cows, which was ailing. He accompanied her, and looking at the animal said, 'Ma bhios i beo bithidh, agus mur a bi basaichidh i.' ('If she lives she will live, and if not she will die.') With that he retraced his steps. Some time after, the minister became ill, and the woman went to see him. In spite of the servant's protest, she forced her way to the minister's bedroom. Looking at him, she said, 'Ma bhios thu beo bithidh, agus mur a bi basaichidh thu.' The minister was so taken aback by his own words being applied to himself that he burst out laughing, which resulted in a growth on his throat bursting, and it soon healed.

An old Trotternish missionary, widely and deservedly respected, was somewhat outspoken in his manner. He received a communication stating that two ministers were to visit the congregation, and requesting that men should be selected to be ordained as elders and deacons. He intimated this to the congregation and added: 'Sgribh mise do'n ionnsaidh na'm bitheadh iad cho eolach oirbh 's a tha mise, nach smuaineachadh iad ni de'n t-seorsa.' ('I wrote them saying, if they knew you as well as I do, they would think of nothing of the kind.')

A visiting missionary entered a house, and could not see his way in, so dark was it. He shouted, 'Nach sibh tha gu buileach dorch 'n so, cha leir dhomh c'ait an cuir mi mo chas.' ('How utterly dark you are here, I can't see where to put my foot.') 'Na'm faiceadh thu e mu'n do chuireadh an uinneag a stigh' ('Had you but seen it before the the window was put in'), came the reply from the darkness within.

During the church conflicts on union or separation, there was a meeting to register the 'ayes' and 'nos'. There was a large concourse of people, and several of the clergy on either side. An old *bodach*, who was passing by, inquired what was afoot. Some irreverent lounger replied that they were trying to prove that there was no such a personage as the devil. 'Gu ma math a theid leis na daoine coire' ('May it go well with the worthy men'), came from the equally irreverent *bodach*.

Two of the most famous lay preachers in Trotternish were Raonull MacPhadruig (Ronald MacDonald) and Aonghas (Angus) Munro. Once they happened to be guests at the same house. Ronald, who was brimful of humour, was gazing intently into his empty cup. Angus, in horror, asked if he saw anything in the cup. 'Yes,' was the reply. 'What is it?' 'See for yourself,' said the other with a merry twinkle in his eyes, handing over the cup. The other was taken aback when he saw a bird in the enamelling of the cup. On another occasion the friends passed a new-born lamb. Angus remarked how helpless man was at birth in comparison with this lamb. Ronald replied that it would not be so if the humans were clothed and shod before birth! Ronald officiated with the Rev. Roderick MacLeod alternately at Uig and Snizort. The former's addiction to his pipe was a sore to Mr Ruaraidh. Once on his arrival at Snizort he asked if he had dropped the pipe yet. 'Yes,' was the reply. 'I am pleased to know that; when did you?' 'Nuas cul Chinnseaborg' ('Along the back of Kingsburgh'), was the reply. *Sgriob drama*, the tickling of the upper lip, is a sure portent of getting a dram.

During the mutual eligibility church troubles, an old deacon could not decide for himself to which side he would adhere. Being pressed, he said, 'Ge be air bith toabh air am bi maighstir Lamon agus Raonull, bithidh mise.' ('Whichever side Mr Lamont and Ronald are I will be.') This is symptomatic of much of the divisions in church affairs in the Highlands. The great majority cannot explain why they accede, or secede. One cannot help thinking but that the Disruption was a disaster for the Highlands.

6 EARLY SCHOOLS AND OLD TEACHERS

The parish schools were presumably built at the same time as the parish churches. These were modest buildings. Generally the school room was below, and the dwelling house above. Heating was procured by each pupil bringing a peat to the school. Of the old dominies the writer once knew none survive. These old teachers sent their pupils direct to the university, where they gave a good account of themselves. Mr Murdo MacDonald spent a lifetime in Portree, in a modest building, dwarfed by the present elaborate pile. He was a striking specimen of the old-time dominie. A son was the Rev. Colin MacDonald of Rogart, a famous preacher, and often dubbed 'the Spurgeon of the North'. Another notable teacher was Mr MacLean of Braes. He gave three sons to the ministry of the Church of Scotland – Rev. John Kenneth MacLean, Olrig; Rev. George Murcoch MacLean, Tayport; and the Very Rev. Dr Norman MacLean of St Cuthberts, Edinburgh, and ex-moderator of the General Assembly. In the Snizort parish school was a Mr Ninian MacKenzie. He was not long appointed when he became insane. As the tenure of office was *ad vita aut culpa*, the parish had to pay the usual salary to his guardians for more than half a century. The writer met him once. He was very aged then, quite silly, but harmless, always crooning snatches of song. He was succeeded by Mr Donald Fraser, afterwards of Glenelg. In Kilmuir there was a Mr

Montgomery, a native of Lewis. Mr Donald Nicolson, a native of Skye, followed, and spent a lifetime there. The salaries in these schools were very modest, and paid by the proprietors. In Stenscholl parish, Mr Archibald Cameron, a native of Moulin, Perthshire, passed his teaching life, and died there. The salary in this instance was paid from the exchequer.

Before and after 1872 most of these schools were added to, or new schools erected, to provide accommodation for the pupils. The problem now is to provide pupils for the accommodation. The EC and FC erected schools where required, and often where not required, ingraining in their children their own miserable church divisions. That has now happily ceased. The Gaelic schools held sway for many years. The teachers were poorly paid, and had to turn to something outside teaching to supplement their meagre salaries. These schools were low, thatched buildings, providing a minimum of lighting. One society school at Kilmaluaig was a slated house. The teacher was a Mr MacDougall, who retired on the advent of the board school. His teaching life was spent there. Some years after retiring, there was a temporary vacancy in the board school, and Mr MacDougall was asked to take duty till the advent of the appointed teacher. Mr MacDougall found the lack of discipline was beyond him. At last, exasperated by the conduct of the pupils, he opened the door, and ordered them all out, saying, 'Chan 'eil umaibh ach na bruidean. De an t-ioghnadh, nach ann air bainne nam bruidean a chaidh bhur n-arach.' ('You are nothing but brutes. What wonder! Is it not on the milk of brutes you have been reared.')

At Uig there were two church schools, EC and FC. The latter was taught by a Miss MacDonald, the former by Mr Malcolm Morrison, a native of Harris. Mr Morrison was continually in litigation with one or two neighbours. It is a far cry to 1870, when the writer's teaching life began at Uig. The building was a long, low thatched house, above high-water mark, on Uig Bay. One end was the schoolroom and the other the dwelling house. The schoolroom was seated for about fifty. The desks were of a primitive construction, with a pulpit-formed desk for the teacher. The school being a church school, the parish minister annually examined it. The first of HM inspectors was Mr Jolly, and jolly he was not on his first visit. The day was unusually wild, with lashing rain. By the time he got to the hotel, he was drenched. He got a change of clothing, and appeared at the school in knickers, so wide that a leg would encircle the body. He smiled as he saw the teacher regarding his unusual rig, and remarked, 'It had to be that or a kilt.' The salary was £35, with three acres and a cow. There was then no compulsory attendance, yet it was fully as good as post-1872. Many came long distances, some as old as the teacher. The desire to learn was keen. Now if over two miles from a school they must have a car. In one instance children one and a half miles from one school are driven to another three miles distant. Not a vestige of the old school remains. Other teachers, fellow-students of the writer, were the late Mr John MacNab, Kilmuir, and the late Mr Alexander Mackenzie of Snizort.

Going to church

IV

REFLECTIONS AND SOME OLD TRADITIONS

1 THE PAST AND PRESENT

The old-time crofter led a quiet existence, unperturbed by the petty worries of present-day life. His wants were few. Spade cultivation yielded a bountiful crop, amply supplying his frugal needs. The women spun and wove all the required clothing. The men made the footwear, *brogan-ial*, of untanned hides. Flax was grown, and the linen requirements were manufactured. The drover periodically went his rounds and bought his cattle. The crofter ground his own corn in his quern. He produced his own fuel. He required no fire-lighters. The ends of some peats were thrust in the red-hot ashes, and smouldered ready for next morning's fire. The crofter's fire never goes out. His house was his own. What if the accommodation was limited, was he not more than compensated by his open surroundings? Game was not so closely preserved in those old days, and the moor supplied a variety in the menu. So also did fish from river, loch, or sea, if the latter were contiguous. As his needs were few, his labour was not excessive. He carefully cultivated the land, beginning in winter, as weather permitted, laying the soil open to be pulverised by the beneficial action of frost and rain. With the money he got for his cattle, he purchased the simple necessary implements of his calling, laying the major part by. It would surprise what amounts were thus saved. In the old days sheep were milked several times after the lambs were weaned. This milk was made into a large cheese. This, besides providing a substantial article of food, saved the sheep from udder trouble. The lambs were clipped, and the fine wool went to make finer articles of clothing. Both processes have long since been discontinued.

During the long winter nights people sat round the peat fires, the old men related the old tales and legends, handed down from father to son, at the same time twisting heather into thatching rope, and the older women were busy at the spinning wheel, or it might be singing the old songs. Pipe music obtained in all the hamlets. Repairing to one of the barns, some nights would be passed in dancing. With plain food, and pure water, ideal surroundings, and healthy outdoor exercise, these old crofter families lived a cheerful vigorous life. Such a life compares very favourably with that of the city dwellers.

The present-day crofter does not make the same use of the land. He depends more on outside labour by himself or members of his family. So the land deteriorates. His standard of living is higher, the croft does not supply it. The outside labour has to make up the deficiency. If that fails, his position is not to be envied.

The old historical houses of Trotternish could furnish many tales of the long-past history, now wrapped in legendary lore. As the clan feuds ceased, the fighting instincts got a wider field. Many thousands of hardy warriors won undying fame on the battlefields of the empire. From the Peninsular War, many veterans returned, but the majority lie under 'the blood-red fields of Spain'. From the Crimean War and Indian Mutiny came the same tale – many perishing, the few returning. These were the twenty-one years' service men. Ashanti took its toll. In America also, Trotternish soldiers fell in the capture of Ticonderago and Quebec. Captain Donald MacDonald led and guided the ascent of the Heights of Abraham, was the first man over the top, silenced the sentry, and the British forces were on the plain before the French were aware of anything untoward happening. The Royal Emigrant Regiment was largely composed of Trotternish men, Captain Allan MacDonald, Flora MacDonald's husband, and his sons serving together with many who emigrated before and with them to Carolina. The 76th MacDonald Regiment was largely recruited in Trotternish.

The South African War took its own toll of our young manhood. In the Great War, the 51st Highland Division were worthy descendants of the men whom Pitt called from the mountains of the north. The many war memorials bear sad testimony to the supreme sacrifice made by Trotternish boys. At the square at Portree, where the army of James V was marshalled, stands a war memorial bearing sad testimony to the price paid by the village in the Great War (1914–1918).

The writer remembers when there were but three slated houses in the Staffin district. There are now sixty or seventy and annually the number is added to. The 'black' houses are still in a majority, but the houses that reared the gallant boys of the 51st Division were not to be despised. I once heard an old auctioneer at a sale declare he remembered when there were but three teapots in the Staffin district, which had a population of eight hundred, and I spoke to an old merchant, who went yearly to Glasgow for his stock, bringing five or six pounds of tea, part of which sometimes remained unsold, when he went for the following year's supply. Progress in tea drinking far outstripped progress in housing.

2 RIVERS

Of the rivers of Trotternish the Snizort is the longest in Skye. The Haultin, Romisdale, Rha, Conon, and Staffin are all of considerable length. The rest are mere burns or *allts*, some running into the larger streams. Some of these *allts*, crystal clear, have their sources in gushing springs, and sparkle along their rocky beds, down the hillside, cheerfully musical. They are even refreshing to look at as they glitter along their silvery course. On the east side are Allt Garbh, Allt Glas, Allt Fionnaghlas, Allt Rig. At times they become raging torrents, but, however much flooded, they preserve their transparency. On the west there are none of these rills; those that are there are dark and sluggish. Most of the rivers are good fishing streams. There is a tradition of the *each-uisge* inhabiting Loch Dursco. It was said he frequently passed along the Grimiscaig to the Staffin River to gambol in the deep dark pools at Bugha nan Each. Well might the credulous connect the monster with these pools. More repulsive and evil-looking pools could not be imagined, suspicious and dark as Hades. The bed of the Staffin abounds with the pearl-mussel, and pearl-fishers occasionally visit it, and are more or less successful.

3 HILLS

The vast chain of the Trotternish Hills from the Storr in the south to the Quiraing and Sron Bhiornal in the north, may be viewed from the roadside. They vary in height from the Storr (2,343 feet), to Beinn Edra and Quiraing (2,000 feet), to Sron Bhiornal (1,600 feet). Abrupt and craggy on the east, they slope gently to the west, and present a splendid vista of mountain scenery seldom to be met with elsewhere. Verdant to their summits, they slope steeply downward till their bases are merged in the wide spreading moorland beneath. At intervals the chain is broken by depressed *bealachs* of varying breadth and form, from the narrow and difficult Bealach nam Fiadh to the wide-spreading Bealach Ollasgairte through which the road from Uig to Staffin runs. The numerous *bealachs* are short-cuts from east to west. The *bealachs* and hills, like the corries, have their nebulous ghostly residents, who at certain times assumed a material embodiment, and roamed at large, over and about their invisible spiritual abodes. The ghostly visitor to Quiraing, to which I already alluded, and the *colunn gun cheann* of Beinn Edra are some of the ghostly visitants, credited as appearing in these favoured haunts, by the old folks of past ages. The corries of Trotternish are many and varied in extent and form. They are invariably green, and afford excellent pastures and sheltering for sheep. In the olden times the wild cattle were grazed for six months in the corries Coire nan Laogh and Coire an Sheagaich. They have a gloom and glamour of their own, inspiring an awesome feeling into the minds of those intruding into their depths.

Each had its own legend, weird yet fascinating, handed down from generation to generation, and recounted round the peat fires of the long wintry nights. In the solemn stillness, the deepening gloom, and the profound solitude and silence bereft of all life, one cannot but have the expectancy that those legendary tales of the fireside may materialise, and the hobgoblins of the legend, fully credited by the people of old, may spring into being. What is true of one corrie applies to most. Some of the corries of Trotternish are: Coire Fuar, Coire Faoin, Coire Fhinn, Coire Sgamadail, Coire nam Fiadh etc. When the summering in the corries ceased, the *airigh* (sheiling) came into being, and carried on till it, in its turn, also ceased. They, like the corries, had their own apparitions, which also were fully credited, and even today the belief in these is still held.

4 MEMORIAL CAIRNS

Throughout Trotternish, on either side, there are numerous cairns, marking places of tragedy or death by misadventure. Originally piled on the discovery, they were reverently preserved by passers-by adding a stone to the cairn. This was meant as a mark of respect for the dead, and boded no good to the passer-by who failed to pay his tribute. Among many others, there are two marking the double tragedy to the bridal party at Loch Corcusdal, to which allusion has already been made. The practice is still continued. A few months ago a party passing the loch placed a stone on one cairn, and deviated from their path to do the same to the other, believing respect to the one was disrespect to the other, if not equally treated. Of this party one was the grandson of the groomsman on the fatal occasion. Among others, besides the Carnan Mairi already alluded to, there is Carnan 'ic an t-Sagairt (Priest's Son) near Kilmuir, where the boy was found dead, and Cairn na-h-Ighinn, near Kensaleyre. Besides these artificial cairns, there are scores of others, though not literally cairns. They are but a conglomeration of rocks and boulders, piled up in a shapeless mass, one over the other, detached from the cliffs above by the forces of nature through the centuries.

5 THE CROFTER AT HOME

As a model of courteous manners the Skye crofter has scarcely a superior, and Lord Napier paid a graceful tribute to this trait of the Highland character, in an otherwise diversified personality. Without humility he respectfully addresses his superiors, and in his intercourse with his social equals he is affable and friendly. While shy and somewhat reserved with strangers, he quickly recovers his inborn disposition, and responds frankly to the greeting of the stranger. Skye hospitality is proverbial, and no part exceeds in warmth of welcome and kindness than is met with along the glens and wayside roads of Trotternish. The stranger need not fear overstaying his visit, and is invariably requested to call again. It has been alleged that the crofter is a lazy, easy-going person. Nothing could be farther from the truth. There are black sheep in every community, but the average crofter has a life of unremitting toil. As his is an open-air life, there must be periods of enforced idleness, and these have to be overcome by additional effort. There is no question of a seven- or eight-hour day in his vocation, nor is there any *ca' canny*. His hours are from dawn to dusk. His labour begins in the early spring – delving, sowing, planting, harrowing take up his time; peat-cutting, fitting, stacking and carrying home absorb a part. Weeding, hoeing, sheep shearing and dipping, tending cattle etc. bring him to harvesting of oats and potatoes. His stacks and houses have to be made secure from winter gales. His sole relaxation is a change of labour. Housing, feeding and tending cattle keep him fully employed during the short winter days. The laziness is alleged by persons utterly ignorant of the crofter and crofter life. Where the family circumstances permit, he may engage in seasonal employment away from home. While wresting a living from uncongenial soil and adverse atmospheric conditions, there is the fact that he is master in his own house. His surroundings, pure open air and the purest of water, invigorate his nerves.

His house, though mean from without, is cosy and warm within, and he has a perfect disinfectant in the smoke, so much derided.

Though the old-time *ceilidh* is a thing of the past, the long winter nights have a charm for young and old. The crofter is possessed of a fund of quiet pawky humour. Gathered by the peat fire, sally and repartee keep all in high spirits. The sarcastic is avoided. Songs with popular chorus are lustily sung. A dreamer of the past is the crofter, in which he would fain penetrate the closed vistas of mystery, and of the future, in which he would equally rend the limiting veil. Much has been made of the drinking habits of the Gael. Whatever it may have been in the past, he, as a class, can now compare favourably with any class in the country. Despite his discomforts, and varying returns for labour, the crofter is in an infinitely better position, social and material, than a similar city class, and a greater asset to the country.

In winter the mountains and hills present a vivid contrast to the peaceful aspect of the serene summer time. They are wrapt in the sombre gloom of the dark winter. Clouds float along, speeded by the howling, whistling wind, enveloping hill and mountain from summit to base, and spread over the wide moorland. The merciless nipping rain pours down in torrential fury. The mountain streams become turbulent torrents, raging and rushing down the steep declivity, as if eager to discharge their quota to the rivers beneath, which in turn rush onward, overflowing banks, and carrying obstructive obstacles in their train. The city dweller might well be depressed by the gloomy scene. To the Highlander it speaks of times past. In the onward rush he finds a parallel to the traditional charge of his ancestors on many battlefields, and he recalls the stirring fights for clan and country. It may be a hail storm biting the face. It may be a blinding snow storm, a veritable blizzard blocking each *bealach*, filling the corries with impassable snow-wreaths. The sea responds, and the surf-beaten shore resists the rolling, grinding waves. It is a scene of wild grandeur, which finds an appropriate affinity in the mind of the Gael as he gazes on such a panorama, unfolded by the elements, and to his house and peat-fires he turns, envying none.

6 EARLY FORMS OF LIGHTING

Lighting was common in the old days by splits of bog pine, and a clear good light they gave. This may have been the origin of the saying, 'Gleann

Min Moireastan far nach ith na coin na coinnlean.' ('Fair Glenmoriston where the dogs don't eat the candles.') This mode of lighting in my own early days was common in many parts of the Highlands, and no doubt it is so still. In my early home candles, both dip and mould, were made every winter, but the suet and tallow go now to make the 'dumpling', quite an institution nowadays among the crofters. The old cruisie (one of which I possess) long held sway. Filled with fish oil and wick of the dried piths of rushes, it gave a fairly good light for these days. The cruisie gave way to the paraffin lamp. The old people were very chary in handling the new light. For long, many would not fill the lamp except in the open, and the supply was carefully put away outside. The next stage will be gas, to be ousted in turn by electricity.

The smoker had his steel and flint, and paper saturated with saltpetre. In hot days the concave glass of his old verge, with concentrated focus of sunlight, set alight the paper. His next aid was the fusee match, followed by the modern match. Snuff has entirely disappeared. The last old man whom I knew use it got some tobacco, dried it, and pounded it in the lid of an iron kettle. There was no demand for snuff, and it ceased being stocked.

Inside the croft-house

7 OLD METHODS

The *cas-chrom* is hardly to be seen now, but delving by it was far ahead of the plough for crop-getting. It was surprising what amount two men would turn in a day. The digging was deep, the upturned sod broken, soon pulverised by air and frost, making a perfect seed bed. The old *bodachs* began the work about Christmas, so the soil would benefit by frost and air. Where the *cas-chrom* went, the flail went. The wooden plough gave place to the iron. I just remember seeing one of the former. It looked serviceable.

Cas Chrom – the crooked spade

When herding, the women always carried the *fearsaid* (spindle) and wool, and would have quite a large ball of thread spun by eventime. Though the *fearsaid* was supplanted by the spinning wheel, the former was still used out of doors. Both *fearsaid* and wheel are now out of use. In most houses there is a wheel, but it is rare to see one used, though forty years ago the whirr of the wheel invariably greeted an entrant. Now it is the mill for everything – carding, spinning and weaving. The many native dyes are discarded for 'fairy dyes'. There were close on a dozen weavers in Trotternish within my memory; now I know of none. It is not to the credit of Trotternish women that outside women are now teaching them the art of their mothers. Flax was grown and linen was manufactured up to seventy years ago. The last I saw of this was bundles of flax steeping in water, which was part of the conversion process.

In former times there was great rivalry in cutting the corn. The *'deir bhuana'* was the finish. The *gobhar bhacach* was thrown on the unfinished neighbour's field as a mark of contempt. This was two bands of corn at right angles, tied in the middle, and placed in a prominent position; often several of the finished reapers would go round the fields, placing these. Much of the work was done with the sickle, *corran caol*, and the *corran mor*. When finished, they repaired to the house, where a large basin of *stapag* was awaiting them. The *stapag* was partly churned cream, mixed with a good sprinkling of oatmeal in which several articles were hidden – a coin, button, thimble, etc. The luck was determined by the find. Merry-making followed. There was another practice called 'gainage'. At the first day's work, the first person passing the reapers was encircled with a band of corn, and held tight till he paid for his freedom. The writer was present when no less a person than a brother of Lord Elphinstone, who was resident at the time in the district, was the subject. He was certainly taken aback, but when explained to him, took it in good humour and handed a crown piece to the daring damsel. For some years a commendable practice has set in of everyone who has finished passing to help their neighbour, and so on, till in a few hours all is cut.

8 AN ATROCIOUS INSTITUTION

Little more than two hundred years ago, there existed an enactment of tyranny, unparalleled and more obnoxious than any tax, poll or otherwise, that man could devise. When a man died, the laird's ground officer put in an appearance, and took away the widow's best horse or best cow, even if she had only one. Not only was the animal removed, but for her resistance the unfortunate woman was abused in offensive and obscene terms.

This custom prevailed in Skye as two cases, one from the north and the other from the south, will demonstrate.

A widow in the north end of Skye had her only cow seized. The animal was put into a field along with the ground officer's horse. While he was feasting or dallying in a neighbouring house, the horse and cow were spirited away and secured in a secret place. The ground officer was outraged when he found the horse and cow both gone, and threatened all and sundry with pains and penalties. The reputed local witch appeared on the scene, approached the officer and so terrorised him that he fled and never came back. The horse and cow were brought forth and presented to the widow.

In the south end of Skye, a MacKinnon died and, as usual, the widow's best horse was seized. The widow put up such a resistance that he attacked her to the effusion of blood. The widow's only son was of tender years, but she told the ground officer that she hoped he would grow up to avenge the treatment of his mother. Young MacKinnon grew up to be the finest and strongest man in the parish. In due course, the same ground officer came to a nearby farm on a similar errand, behaving with his usual insolence, and went off with a horse. Young MacKinnon mounted his horse, pursued and overtook him. He demanded the return of the widow's horse, but this was refused and they fought. MacKinnon was victorious and cut off his opponent's head. He rode to the chief's house, bearing the ground officer's head on the point of his dirk. The laird was told that young MacKinnon was outside with big Duncan's head on his dirk, and was shocked to find it was true. But on hearing of the recent proceedings, as well as the cruel treatment of the widow seventeen years previously, he granted the young man a free pardon, and appointed him ground officer. He ordered that never again would a widow be deprived of part of her property. Ground officers as a class were heartily hated. A crofter, giving evidence before Lord Napier's commission, said, 'Yes, we are afraid even of the ground officer's dog.'

9 *COILLE THARABHAIDH*

Before banking facilities were available in Skye, most monetary transactions were carried out in Inverness. This was, until comparatively recent times, attended with dangers and difficulties. On the road to Inverness, at Tarvie, was a dense forest, which from remote times was infested with robbers, who intercepted and preyed upon unprotected travellers. Many years ago, Mr Donald MacLeod of Arnisdale and Kingsburgh was travelling home from Inverness. On the road, he overtook a woman, who asked for a lift. This was readily given, and the journey was resumed, but Mr MacLeod became suspicious of his fellow traveller. Remaining calm, he studied her furtively, and found that he was carrying a bearded man, instead of a helpless woman. Unnoticed, he slipped his plaid over the side of the dog cart. Fumbling about, he glanced backward and remarked that his plaid had dropped out. He stopped and requested his passenger to go back for it. When he was about to pick it up, Mr MacLeod gave his spirited horse his head. The disguised robber realised he had been duped, and was able only to fire some harmless shots after the vanishing dog cart.

MacKinnon of Corry was in need of a sum of money. He was unable to go to Inverness at the time, and had difficulty in deciding whom he should trust to make the journey safely. Calum Ban, one of his retainers, offered his services, provided he was given the white mare, the fleetest in the Corry stable, and a whip. Calum was a half-wit, but endowed with a cunning common to his type. Corry was doubtful, but, knowing Calum's resourcefulness, entrusted him with the matter, and Calum set out. On his way through the wood, he encountered a well-spoken man who conversed with him in a friendly manner. Calum told him of his errand, and he in turn was told of the danger in travelling alone. He arranged to meet Calum on his return on a certain day, and see him to safety. Calum agreed, and continued his journey to Inverness, where he presented Corry's letter.

He was given the parcel of money required, and asked the banker to make up an identical false package, which he placed in the inside pocket of his coat. Calum secured the genuine packet somewhere about his person, and took to the road again. At the appointed place, he met the same man who greeted him in a friendly manner, and they walked on talking freely. At a dark point in the wood, the would-be protector turned suddenly round and, presenting a pair of pistols, demanded Calum's money. Calum pretended to be greatly upset, and called himself a fool to have trusted his fine words. Reluctantly, he handed over the packet from inside his coat, and the robber pocketed it. Calum asked the robber to fire two shots through his coat, so that his master would see that he did not give up his charge without a struggle, and obligingly, the robber did so. With the robber's pistols now empty, Calum leapt into the saddle, gave the whip to the white mare, and was soon out of reach. In due time, he arrived home, and handed Corry the genuine package.

10 SUPERSTITION

The superstitions of the past are now mostly discarded. *Toirt a mach an toraidh* (taking the milk from the cows) was a belief held almost universally, but not quite discredited. I knew quite a sensible man, a church deacon, who, with his wife, went to Nairn to complain to the proprietor of a neighbour who was taking the milk from his cows. The laird's face may be imagined when he heard the cause of their visit. Near here lived an old man whose services were greatly in request all over Skye in 'curing' cows from this witchcraft. His wife succeeded him in the 'trade', which no doubt was a lucrative profession. Though witchcraft is dead, it eked out a lingering existence. Not a great many years ago a crofter lost a cow. Imputing its death to witchcraft, he complained to the factor, who ridiculed the belief in such a fantastic idea of there being any witch. 'Who brought Samuel from his grave?' retorted the man. Presented with a one pound note by the factor he was mollified and went off.

Droch shuil (the evil eye) is yet firmly believed in. I knew a woman who, when herding her cows, saw anyone approaching, turned her back and, facing the cows, kept repeating, 'Dhia gleidh iad' ('God keep them') until the person was well on his way. When a cow is ill, or shows suffering pain, the evil eye was inevitably the cause. The remedy in such a case is to sprinkle the beast with water in which gold and silver is immersed. I saw this remedy quite recently applied. The beast got well, and no doubt about the remedy remained. I knew another case in which, when throwing away the charmed water, the gold ring used was thrown away and lost. I once bought a churn at the sale of the effects of an eminent old minister. Wedged between the stave and the bottom was a sixpenny piece, no doubt to preserve the *toradh* in the cream. The minister I expect would have been ignorant of his women-folk's device. Another belief, still existing, is that it is unlucky to begin cutting corn on Monday. To avoid this, two or three stooks were cut on Saturday eve. 'An obair a nithear Di'luain bithidh i luath no mall.' ('Work done on Monday will be quick or slow.') An old saying and belief was the following:

Chunnaic mi clacharan air garradh toll,
Chunnaic mi seilcheag air lic bha lom,
Chunnaic mi eun-ghabhrag air mullach tom.
Chuala mi chuthag 's gun biadh 'nam bhroinn,
Chunnaic mi searrach 's a chulaobh rium,
'S dh'aithnich mi nach rachadh a' bhliadhna sin leam.

I saw a stone-chitter on a broken dyke,
A snail on a bare ledge,
A snipe on the top of a grass tuft.
I heard the cuckoo before having food,
I saw a foal with his back to me,
And I knew the year to me would not be a prosperous one.

This belief was so strongly engrained that the unfortunate made little attempt to improve his position, believing that all his efforts would be futile, thus strengthening belief in the efficacy of the rhyme.

Even today children and old persons try to avoid some of the above ill-omens. To a seventh son was ascribed a miraculous power of curing certain ailments. The belief I had thought had been extinct. A recent case dispelled my belief. A seventh son was brought from a considerable distance for the ailment of a certain person. The cure, whatever it was, did not materialise, and it is to be hoped the delusion is getting its *quietus*. *Toir an tochd* (removing the stye) of cattle was a most senseless and painful proceeding. A beast showing symptoms of illness was operated on for *tochd*. This consisted in slicing with a razor the inside of an eyelid, and then spitting tobacco juice into the eye.

It is an old belief that the haddock and *carbhain* (carp) are the fishes with which Christ fed the multitude, and the black spots on each side of the fish are the imprints of his fingers. Another old belief is that the flounder was punished with a twisted mouth for mocking other fish! 'Giomach 's rionnach, 's ron, tri seoid a chuain.' ('The lobster, mackerel and seal, the three swiftest in the sea.') The lobster does not look as possessing swiftness, yet it is true. The mackerel is well known for its swiftness, and the seal is capable of seizing such strong swimmers as grilse and salmon. Every year they are trapped in the salmon nets. The otter is fairly numerous along the coast and rivers. A tidy sum is seasonably made by trappers. One of these, on visiting a trap, found in it a large flounder, which the animal caught in the sea and was carrying to its lair.

11 SECOND SIGHT

Taibhsearachd (second sight) is still firmly believed in. I knew an old man who was said to have this. It was believed he had witnessed some terrible scene. True it was that nothing would tempt him to go outside in the darkness. Another young man was afflicted with the same foible. He would not dare go into the darkness without a companion. Lights are seen, it is said, in connection with death. Not many years ago I was one of the bearers of a coffin. It was laid down to enable the bearers to cross a stream. An old man present declared he saw a light on the spot a week previously. Quite a number are credited with *taibhs*, and numerous instances are given, but usually after the event. One night, while a woman was preparing for bed, she happened to look out at a window, and cried in alarm that the byre was alight. Her husband and others rushed to the place, but saw nothing. Next day a girl was killed on the spot at which the light was seen. The writer can vouch for this as he was in the house at the time. The horse is said to have this faculty. An instance was related to me recently. A carter was carting peats from the moss. Suddenly the horse bolted. A week later the man declared the horse bolted from a spot where a funeral party stood to change bearers.

Cup reading is still practised, and the 'initiated' give wonderful and alarming predictions, and it is amusing to see even the young turn their cups and scan earnestly the tea leaves. A small tea stalk floating on a cup predicts the advent of a stranger.

The rowan and elder are widely seen growing round crofter houses; every crofter endeavours to have one or both near his house, believing they afford security to the house and all belongings from evil spirits. The traveller can often see a horseshoe nailed over a door, bringing luck to the house, and warding off the influence of the evil eye. When a coffin is lifted from the chairs on which it is resting, the chairs are turned upside down, and formerly were washed before being again used. When a death occurs in a crofter hamlet, all work is suspended till the dead is carried over the boundary, and this while in the hamlets around people go about their ordinary occupations. In Wales a more practical custom exists. Work goes on as usual, and a day's pay is contributed to the stricken family. No live peat is allowed out of a house until the baby in the house is baptised.

A pious old neighbour woman on her way to a religious service met me while going fishing. I jokingly said to her: 'Faodaidh mise tilleadh, cha bhi 'n t-iasgach ann.' ('I may return as there will be no fishing.') Ever after she invariably shunned a meeting. There was a man and a boy I often went fishing with, and they were careful to drop their lines on the right side, asserting the apostle Peter cast his net from that side. The mermaid and sea serpent myth is still existent; sailors have kept alive the latter. The mermaid is called *maighdean mhara*. I never met anyone who saw the lady, but numbers of people who said others saw her. A Treaslan (Snizort) woman dreamt that she saw her husband and his crew clinging to their upturned boat. She was so impressed with its reality that she went to the relatives of the other men. Neither the men nor boat were ever heard of. This fatality occurred in 1872.

Sacred wells are widely scattered. One is near Loch Sniosdal in Kilmuir.

Invalids in search of health, others in search of luck, drank of its waters, dropped some pin or coin into it, and walked sunwise three times round it. There is another such well in Linicro, Kilmuir, one in Sartle, Tobar na Slainte (Well of Health), and one in Flodigarry. I once was well acquainted with one by the seashore, two miles north of Kyleakin. I forget its name. All parties returning from shellfish-gathering each dropped a shell into it, otherwise there was no luck for the negligent next time.

The itinerant tailor so familiar in the old days has disappeared. The native pedlars are also of the past. Many Trotternish people will recall the last of these, Domhnull Shaw and Lachlann na Ciste. Both confined their itineracy to Trotternish, and were very jealous of any odd pedlar poaching on what they regarded as their sole preserve. Both made their headquarters at Kensaleyre. Donald was a waspish character, his very features were stamped with irascibility. He carried his *bathar* (wares) in an arm basket. When he entered a house he opened up his goods. If nothing was wanted, a hint was given to some one to make some disparaging remark. Donald gave an irate look at the offender, threw his wares in a heap into his basket, and marched out in high dudgeon. Boys sometimes teased him, but it was a dangerous game, as he was not loath to hurl some missile at the offender. Lachlan was the very opposite in demeanour. He carried his stock in a trunk strapped across his shoulders. He carried a variety of wares: clothing, hardware, tobacco etc. He never unduly pressed his goods. He sold tobacco by length, from the tip of the middle finger to the elbow as two ounces. He was more favoured on his rounds than his rival. When he got a new suit he put the old jacket over the new until worn off. Wherever he put up for the night he had his cist (chest) beside him. On one of his rounds through Scorrybreac he was much depressed on his return. He made several journeys across the hill. On each return he was further depressed. It was eventually found that, seeing a man apparently following him and recalling tales of robbery on Scorrybreac, he hid what money he had, and could not again find it. He was a native of Strath, and died at a relative's house in Eyre. The cist was found to contain £87. Where Donald Shaw sprung from was not known.

12 OLD SAYINGS

'Miosa Faoilleich, naoi latha Gearrain, tri latha sguabaig, sud suas air an t-Earrach.' ('Month of the *Faoilleach*, nine days of biting cold, three days of the broom and then up with the Spring.') 'Bu choir do'n Fhaoilleach (tighinn) a steach le ceann nathrach air, agus a' dhol am mach le earball peucaig; ach na'n tigeadh e a steach le ite na peucaig agus a' dhol am mach mar an nathair, no ma thig e a steach mar uan is a' dhol am mach mar leoghann, gabhaidh an Gearran seachd leumannan cuthaich!' ('The *Faoilleach* should come in with a serpent's head, and go out with a peacock's tail; but if it were to come in with the feather of a peacock and go out like the serpent, or if it should come in like a lamb and go out like a lion then the *Gearran* will give seven leaps of madness: that means that these nine days will be a veritable cataclysm.')

Another old saying is, 'Cuach mu Bhrid, ubh mu Innid, eun mu Chaisg, Mur am bi sin aig an fhitheach, bithidh am bas.' ('A nest at St Bride's day, an egg at Shrove Tuesday, a fledgling at Easter. If the raven has not that he will have death.') *Feill Bride* is 13 February, and of old it was considered that half the winter fodder should be in stock. *Feill-Padhruig* was the middle day of Spring. A saying: 'B'fhearr leam creach thighinn air a' bhaile na maduinn mhin an fhaoilleich fhuair.' ('I would prefer a foray on the township rather than a fair warm morning of the cold equinox.') The harvest moon, it was asserted, did not rise so high in the sky, and tarried in its course. This moon is termed *gealach cul nan garaidhean* (behind the dikes moon), and also is called *gealach an abuchaidh* (the ripening moon). Peats were stacked during a waning moon, otherwise they will give more smoke than flame. Sheep were killed at the new moon, otherwise they shrink when cooked.

13 THE SHIELING

More than sixty years ago, the writer had the experience of passing two nights at a sheiling, and what was seen and learned at that time is the following.

Before the migration took place, the men-folk resorted to the locale to repair and refit the huts. These were of turf, with divot-covered roof, thatched with heather, and were disposed to ensure the maximum of shelter. Their dimensions were very limited, but, as life was spent in the open with the heather-scented breezes blowing about, the cramped accommodation mattered little. Then came the 'flitting'. The men carried any necessary articles, and shepherded the cattle, and the women the milk vessels, bedding and food. The cattle, on the rich succulent grass of the dells and hillsides, gave a markedly increased flow of milk. The young women milked, accompanying the work with a song or ditty suited to the operation. The milk was set in a different hut to the living one, and butter and curds were made in due course. The shieling life, which lasted for three months, was looked forward to in keen anticipation, and no wonder, as it constituted a welcome change from the labour of spring work, and a healthy pleasant picnic midst the solitudes of nature. This practice at the period referred to was fast dying out. The older people remained at home, and the homes were visited daily by one or other of the campers. This does not refer to Trotternish, but to a more secluded part of the far north. As far as Trotternish is concerned, the shieling life had passed into oblivion long before this period, and nothing remains of the old shielings but the names – Airigh an Easain, Airigh Ghrimeasaig, Airigh Dhonnchaidh, Airigh Neill, Airigh Mhor etc.

14 EMIGRATION

While men of the crofter class adventured forth in great numbers, perhaps in greater numbers than Lowland Scots, it was different to a great extent with women. The writer knew a woman who died aged eighty-six, and who never had seen Portree, which was within six miles of her home. This is not an exceptional case, and many instances may be gathered from the following, related to me many years ago. Two women had a bitter quarrel. Abusive epithets and recrimination followed fast and furious. At length one termagant addressed her opponent thus, 'Shiubhail mi deas is tuath, an ear 's an iar, 's rainig mi an Cadha-Ruadh am Bracadal 's bean do theanga cha do thachair riamh orm.' ('I travelled south and north, east and west, I reached Ca-roy in Bracadale [three miles distant], and a woman of your tongue I never met.') Few women of the early part of two generations back saw a train. True, a number repaired to the harvest fields of the Lothians, 'Loudai' as they so named it, and numbers were recruited for the jute mills of Dundee. It is all different now. The Education Act of 1872, and following acts, supplied the equipment, the impetus, and incentive to see more of the world, and seek more congenial employment in the cities of the south, and the pleasures thereof, than the harassing monotonous toil that awaited them on the croft. From 1872 onwards, almost as soon as compulsory education took its hold, the migration southwards set in, and has continued since in increasing numbers. Domestic service absorbs the majority, while other occupations await the better educated.

Of later years, very many have gone further afield to Australia, New Zealand, the USA and Canada. There is quite a colony of Trotternish girls and young men in Toronto. They are very mindful of the homes they left, and, as a rule, when within reach, they annually revisit the old home, but have lost any desire to settle down again.

Many of both sexes marry and make their home in the south, and so the homeland population dwindles. This is vividly shown by the decrease of school population. The writer in 1879 opened the local school with a roll of ninety-six; it is now fourteen. A neighbouring school had a roll of two hundred; there are now less than fifty. It is the same all over Skye, and the Highlands generally. What is the remedy? It is difficult to see any. While the land, generally, is now under crofts and smallholdings, the population continues to dwindle. There are very few economic holdings, and only by the help of members of the family in occupations elsewhere could the occupiers exist. The homing instinct is strong, but falls short of again settling on the croft. There is an absence of the social pleasures and entertainments which appeal to the young. The bagpipes and other music, instrumental or vocal, are tabooed, and innocent dancing is condemned. What wonder then that young men going south, and freed from the restraints of the homeland, plunge into social life, which may lead to degradation and degeneracy, and often does. The honesty of the objectors to secular enjoyment is unquestionable, but the repression unquestionably leads too often to moral wreckage. Let the young then enjoy, nay encourage them to enjoy, these innocent enjoyments, appealing to healthy youth, and forbid them not, while they are still within the ambit and genial influence of the home. Nothing but good would be the result.

Mo chride bruite 's deoir le m' shuilean,
A falbh gu duthaich gun surd, gun sheol,
Far nach faic mi cluaran, no noeinean guanch,
No fraoch no luachair, air bruaich na lon.

My heart, bruised, and tears in my eyes,
Going to a land without enthusiasm or direction,
Where I shall not see a thistle or a dainty daisy,
Or heather or rushes on the banks of the streams.
     William Mackenzie, 1934.

15 SOLDIERS OF THE EMPIRE

Skye, as is well known, contributed to the Napoleonic wars ten thousand common soldiers, six hundred captains, and many officers of higher rank. An early memory is seeing the old veterans going quarterly to Portree to draw their pensions and where, no doubt, they fought their battles over again. Many retired officers occupied the farms of Sartle, Balmeanach, Scorr, Lachasay, Feall, etc. The widow of Captain Somhairle (Samuel) Feall, a centenarian, was living in 1886, and was visited by Charles Fraser Macintosh, MP, who had an interesting chat with the old lady. Another Peninsular War veteran named his first-born son, Rowland Hill, after his divisional general, and this Rowland Hill MacDonald filled a high position in the post office, probably through the general's influence with his kinsman of penny-post fame. Another old Peninsular veteran was Murdo Nicolson. Oft as a boy I listened to his thrilling tales of battle. Murdo described Badajos as the devil's own work. The Pyrennean passes were like a bit of home, and Toulouse was easy going. He would sometimes get excited, start, and with military step march back and fore. He came through unscathed except for a bruised leg in a charge of the French cavalry at Waterloo. Murdo was a fine type of the old-time soldier, six feet high, straight as a rod, lean and wiry.

Many of the past generations will remember Somhairle Ban (Fairhaired) who lived at the crossroads at Borve. He was a Crimean and Indian Mutiny veteran. His forbears were evicted from Borve when that part of Skirinish was cleared. Samuel would be very young when that took place. On his discharge he built a house in the old home. He set up a weaving loom. Both he and his wife became expert weavers and, as they succeeded each other on the weaving stool, the work was continuous. He was the last of his calling in that part of Skye.

Sergeant John Nicolson was another veteran who returned to spend his closing years in his native Eilean a' Cheo. To the close of his life, he retained the bearing and step of a well-trained soldier. Climbing the heights of the Alma, John's headgear was shot off his head. There was no question of recovery; Sir Colin Campbell's orders were strict – to pay no heed to fallen comrades until the action was over. Never was a commander more loved by the men serving under him than was Sir Colin. Often did the writer hear John Nicolson speak of the delight of the men when they found they were again to be serving under Sir Colin in the Indian Mutiny.

He remembers well John's return from the wars, bronzed, brown as a mulatto. Some days later, John's nephew appeared in school, his jacket adorned with a row of the brass buttons of the 42nd, to the envy of every other pupil. John married in Tote, where descendants reside.

Alexander MacPherson was another of these old-time soldiers. Passing through the Crimean campaign, he was drowned in the Hooghly, at the disembarkation of the troops being rushed to the relief of Lucknow.

Another 42nd soldier from Trotternish was Donald Dubh (black) MacDonald. He was always to the front when daring deeds had to be done, often disappearing in the dark and returning with accurate information on the enemy's disposition and strength. He was in the Egyptian Campaign under Abercromby in 1801. The British were facing a strong position held by the French. The officer giving commands was too slow for Donald and he shouted at the pitch of his voice, 'No prime and load, but charge baiglets (bayonets)!' The whole column, stirred by Donald's unexpected shout, with one accord sprang up, swept over the sand-dunes to the French position, carried it with cold steel and captured the whole garrison. Breaches of discipline were overlooked in Donald's case, as his example was a valuable asset to the morale of his unit. He was brought before his commanding officer, his face blackened by the smoke of battle and his bayonet reeking red with French blood, but all that was said to him was, 'It's all right, Donald.' 'It's very all right, sir,' replied Donald. It is uncertain whether Donald fell later at Quatre Bras or Waterloo, where he was engaged; at any rate, there is no certain account of his return to his native Trotternish.

Another old Trotternish soldier was Donald Graham, who fought in the Crimea and the Indian Mutiny, where he lost an arm. He returned home and spent his declining years as a shepherd.

Another veteran of the past was Angus MacMhurchaidh (son of Murdoch). He was an original soldier of the Cameron Highlanders, the regiment raised by that grim, redoubtable old warrior, Allan Cameron of Erracht. Angus became an officer in the regiment and followed its fortunes until his retirement from active service. He was thrice married; his first wife is said to have been a sister of Allan Cameron. Asked by a neighbour which wife he liked best, he replied, 'She who brought me rank and honour.' He had a son, Martin, who went to America. Angus died in Valtos where the ruin of his last abode is still seen, covered with moss and grass.

Another of these fighting clansmen was Maol-Moire MacInnes. He was co-eval with Aonghas MacMhurchaidh. He also attained commissioned rank in the Scots Legionaries, fighting in the Low Countries, and was, at one time, attached to a British corps. It is related of him that, after a certain battle, a very considerable number of prisoners was taken. The difficulty was how to transfer them to the base camp, as they were too numerous to be escorted by the number who could be spared from the fighting line. Maol-Moire was appealed to, and undertook the task with the few men allotted to him. He ordered the prisoners to be lined up facing outwards. He and his men went along the line cutting each man's braces. That done, the prisoners were marched off, each man holding up his trousers. Maol-Moire delivered the prisoners and was complemented on his ingenuity. After many long years of service, he returned home to the hamlet Brechry, where his descendants lived until the beginning of this century.

16 THE ORIGINALS

Any account of Trotternish is not complete without some notice of the wandering fraternity of semi-lunatics in Kilmuir. They were not beggars in reality. They wandered widely, and were welcomed and entertained along their route. Iain Ghilista, William MacGiorman, Alastair MacGiorman, Gilleasbuig Aotrom etc. The first named always kept to the shore, and left it only to get food and refuge for the night. Iain had a spice of revenge in his nature. He came upon some fishermen, and asked for some herring, which at the time they were shaking from their nets. He was told to clear out. On his return in the darkness he launched the boat in question, rowed along the coast, and landed at Mogstad, a distance of twelve miles, leaving the boat on the shore, till secured by someone who had seen it. William was a quiet, inoffensive being. His peculiarity was that of leaving his place of refuge for the night, and, after walking a mile or so, he suddenly retraced his steps to near his starting point. When asked how he lost a thumb, he would reply, 'Crubag a luaidh,' repeated often a dozen times ('crab, my dear'). Alastair was about the last of the fraternity. He was a trustworthy but erratic messenger. A proud man was Alastair when presented with a coat on the arm of which 'Kilmuir messenger' told his profession. When in church, as he often was, he sat on the steps at the pulpit door, and his wide restless grey eyes kept roaming over the church, very trying to the sedateness of the congregation.

At a neighbouring church a gentleman remarked to him that he was of the other church, to which came the reply: 'I am of this church for my body, and of the other for my soul.' Asked what two things he liked best, 'Alaire air an latha agus banais air an oidhche,' was the quick reply. ('A funeral by day and a wedding by night.') Meeting Alastair on the road, his hand was stretched out with his snuffbox before he was within one hundred yards. He had a holy terror of boys, and would go miles out of his way to avoid them. A minister in Kilmuir sent him to Portree with two young pigs in a bag. He was warned in speaking to the gentleman to always address him as 'sir'. If the minister gave him precise instructions, Alastair amusingly amplified them. Delayed somehow, it was midday on Sabbath when passing Snizort. Alarmed at the appearance of some boys, he rushed into the church. The minister requested someone to put the poor man out. Alastair retorted, 'I will go out if you bring in the devils who are out.' He, however, got out. Scared at the occurrence, the boys had disappeared and Alastair resumed his journey. Arriving at Portree, he addressed the gentleman thus: 'Sir minister, sent sir me, to sir you, with sir *muc* (pig), in sir poke.' Gaelic readers will translate for themselves. Alastair often accompanied the late Mr MacIver, minister of Kilmuir, carrying his coat and bag. Mr MacIver was seen to laugh heartily at something Alastair said. It was thus: 'B'fhearr leam, a Mhinistir, gu'n robh mi coltach ruibh.' 'Carson Alasdair?' 'Bhitheadh mo lon's m' aodach, mo dheagh leabadh, 's mo shanaoisean cinnteach.' ('I wish, minister, I was like you.' 'Why Alastair?' 'My food, my clothing, my good bed, and my snuff would be sure.')

Gilleasbuig Aotrom was a cosmopolitan as regards a home. He wandered all over Skye and many parts of the mainland. Innumerable are the tales of his tricks and wit. He played his pranks on friends and foes alike. Even MacKinnon of Corry, under whose protection he roamed inviolate, was not absolved. At a time when the farm grieve was lying seriously ill, a loud knocking was heard at the door of Corry House. Of the maid who opened the door, Gilleasbuig inquired: 'Am bheil Lachlainn a stigh.' ('Is Lachlan in?') The maid hurried away, and Corry appeared. 'O, mo naire (shame), Lachlainn, your grieve is on his death-bed, and you have in your press what will save him.' 'What will save him?' asked MacKinnon. 'A good stiff dram,' was the reply. Corry departed, and quickly returned with the best whisky he had in the house. Gilleasbuig did not go far when Corry called out, 'You rascal, my grieve will never taste that whisky, you will drink it yourself.' 'Deeply would I regret that your mother's son should be a liar,' replied Gilleasbuig, on which he drank to Lachlan's health. Handing back the glass, he promised that the grieve should get the next. On one occasion Gilleasbuig was at Portree pier, where there was a boat with a catch of cod. He asked the fishermen for one, and met with a surly refusal. Watching his opportunity, he stole off with one. Going to the village, he sold the fish for a shilling, saying he himself would clean the fish. This he repeated at several houses. Returning to the pier, with the fish concealed behind him, he waited till the man was bending over his fish in the boat, when he threw the cod with some force on the man's back, saying, 'There's your cod, if you make as much of it as I did, it will be a dear cod in the end.' He always attended cattle markets, and his great delight was to set all the dogs afighting. Even on Sundays he would provoke the shepherds' dogs at the church door to fight. Once, while at Broadford, Corry met Gilleasbuig, who was munching a bone along the road. Corrie said to him, 'You should think shame of yourself going along the road as you do. Give that bone to the first dog you meet.' 'Ah well, you better take it, as I may not meet another dog.'

From the minister of Bracadale he got a note to a shoemaker to make him a pair of shoes. The shoes were got. Gilleasbuig repaired to the manse, saying the shoemaker would not give him the boots till he got payment. The unsuspecting good old man gave him the money, and Gilleasbuig went off with the boots and money. This was only discovered when the shoemaker sent in his account. On another occasion he arrived very late at the manse. All had retired except the minister, who was in his study. He told him there was no-one to make a bed for him, but he could be warm and comfortable in the hay-loft. They went out, and the minister told him to get up the ladder. 'No, you get up first, and see that it is as you say.' The minister did so. Gilleasbuig took away the ladder, saying, 'Take your fill of it, if it is as good as you say', went in, and slept on a sofa, and was far on the road ere the minister was released from his enforced quarters.

His wanderings were not confined to Skye. On one occasion he chanced to be passing the Kintail church. It was Sabbath, and the service was going on. The horse of one of the worshippers was grazing by the church. Gilleasbuig tied the bell rope to the horse's tail, and hid in a thicket to watch the development. As the horse moved on, the bell rang wildly. The startled congregation rushed out, expecting to find some supernatural phenomenon, while Gilleasbuig grinned in the thicket above. He was always about when the lairds and farmers had their 'ordinary' at the hotel after markets. Entering the room, Corry asked him where he came from. 'From Hell,' came the startling reply. 'What are they doing there?' 'Just what they are doing here, taking in the rich and keeping out the poor.' At another 'ordinary' he watched the punch-bowl taken in. With two herring on a plate he followed, and placed it by the gentleman next the bowl. 'Where are you going with that, take it away at once.' 'There it is,' said Gilleasbuig, dropping the herring in the bowl. The bowl was taken away. Gilleasbuig was waiting for it. He poured the contents in a jug, and he and his fellow-loungers made merry over it. Whatever he got by tricks or gratuity he always shared with others. Any question of punishment would raise the resentful ire of the most influential people in the island. A violent lunatic was being removed to an asylum. Gilleasbuig looked at the man, and said, 'Na'm bitheadh an cuthach ceart ort-sa bhitheadh t-aran fuinte.' ('Had you the right madness bread would be secure.') Such are some of the many tales of Gilleasbuig Aotrom. The minister he tricked was a Mr Souter, who was in some way a chamberlain to MacLeod. The following, I much suspect, was Gilleasbuig's own composition:

Nuair a theid e do'n chubaid,
Ni e urnuigh bhios gleusta,
Bithidh cuid dhi an Gaidhlig,
Is pairt dhi 'na Beurla,
Bithidh cuid dhi an Laideann,
'S pairt dhi an Greigis,
'S a chuid nach tuig cach dhi,
Bheir e gaire air Fear Gheusta.

When he goes to the pulpit,
He will make a skilful prayer,
Some of it will be in Gaelic,
And some in English,
Some of it will be in Latin,
And part in Greek;
And what the rest do not understand,
Will make the laird of Gesto laugh.

Of another minister, many years ago, who was inordinately absent-minded, the following is related. Once in the pulpit he fumbled about but could not find his sermon. The beadle watched his difficulty, and to the amusement of the congregation, cried out, 'Try between the cushion and the seat.' Returning to Portree, he and his wife put up at one of the hotels. Early next morning he yoked his dog-cart and was some miles on the road when he discovered the absence of his wife. Returning to the hotel he found her anxiously waiting for him to turn up.

I once knew a man who went by the sobriquet 'Nasaret'. At the Disruption he made himself conspicuous, or rather ridiculous, in his blatant denouncing of the 'moderates'. His sole and only argument was, 'An tig ni math sam bith a Nasaret?' ('Can anything good come out of Nazareth?') So 'Nasaret' stuck. Some years after, he approached the 'moderate' minister for some favour. Having granted his request, the minister twitted him about his old parrot cry, and he said, "S ann bha an cuthaich air daoine an uair sin.' ('Men were mad then.')

17 OLD MEN WHO HAVE QUITTED LIFE'S STAGE:
Their Humorous Sayings and Doings

Two neighbours in Uig, both intelligent men, were sure, whenever they met, to spend some time in arguing some point, usually in scripture, a theme of argument dear to the heart of the Gael. They were so engaged one day, each entrenched in his own opinion, and neither would give way. An old saying is, 'An car a tha 's an shenna mhaide, 's deachair a thoirt as.' (''Tis difficult to straighten the twist in an old stick.') While they were so engaged, they espied another old man coming towards them. They mutually agreed to refer their point of dispute to him, whom both admitted to be their mental superior. The newcomer heard the dispute, smiled at the disputants, and remarked as he passed on, 'O fhearaibh, fannibh anns an tanalachd far an grunnaich sibh.' ('Oh men, stay in the shallows where you can wade.')

In Kilmuir, an old man of ninety lay apparently dying. His wife anxiously inquired what she could give him to sustain or help to maintain his strength. A kindly neighbour, sitting by the bed-side suggested a cup of gruel. This was prepared and brought to the patient. On seeing the contents of the cup, he exclaimed with a scowl: 'Thoir leat do bhrochan tana. B'e sin am biadh do dhuine tha triall air an astar dheireannach?

Thoir do m' ionnsuidh-sa buala broise.' ('Take away your thin gruel. What sort of food is that for a man who is going on his last journey? Bring me a bowl of brose.')

In Kilmuir there once lived a worldly old bachelor, Iain Ruadh (Red John), who had two spinster sisters, equally worldly. Iain died, and when spring-time came, the two spinsters set about preparing their graith for the spring work. One of them took down a horse-collar, which was in much need of repair, and remarked to her sister, 'Dh' fhaodadh e bhi air a' bhreid so a charadh mu'n do d' imich e.' ('He might have mended this collar before he went.')

Some sheep-worrying happened in a Staffin township and, as no trace of the culprit dogs could be found, the aid of the burly local constable was invoked. He went over the whole hamlet, examining each dog in turn. He came to Lachlan Mor, the oldest *bodach* in the township.

Constable: A bheil cu agad? (Have you got a dog?)

Lachlan: Tha cu agam. (I have a dog.)

Constable: Thoir a mach an so e. (Bring it out here.)

Constable (after examining the dog): Tha e n'as reamhaire na bu chor dha bhi leis an onair. (It is fatter than it should be with honesty.)

Lachlan: Tha baltag math suilc ortsa fhein, an ann leis a mheirle a thuair thu e? (You have a good covering of fat on yourself, did you get it by thieving?)

Up to forty or fifty years ago, many men went to the east coast fishing. They were share fishermen. Some seasons might be remunerative and some the reverse. During one bad season, an old man was very concerned at the outcome for his family. He asked a companion to write a letter to his wife for him. After several items were put down, he asked that he write that they were having a good season. 'But that is not true.' 'Never mind, put it down. When it reaches home, the meal merchant will advance all my family's requirements.'

An old Kilmaluag man had the misfortune of being frequently before the sheriff for trivial misdemeanours. The kindly old sheriff, seeing him before him once again said, 'A bheil thu 'n so a rithist?' ('Are you here again?') 'Tha a Shiorram, agus gach uair tha mi 'n so, tha sibhse ann romham.' ('Yes Sheriff, and each time I am here, you are here before me.')

One hot July day, an old *bodach* was wending his way home from the moors. He called at a house on his way and asked for a drink. He was given a bowl of water, when he was expecting a liberal libation of milk to quench his thirst. Handing back the vessel, he said, 'Gu ma pailt sin agaibh ged a ruigeadh e na sparran.' ('May that be plentiful with you should it reach the rafters.')

A certain ambitious man was desirous of bettering his position. To this end, against the advice of his wife, he bought a number of young cattle. Unfortunately for him, prices dropped heavily and he lost badly. To his wife he said, 'You would get a stirk today for an old song.' 'Yes,' retorted his wife, 'and you would sell it for the chorus.'

Four old Culnancnoc *bodachs* went a-fishing in a small boat, setting out on a fine day. Suddenly a storm arose and it was upon them before they could get their lines and anchor up. The oars were unshipped but they made little or no progress. 'Gairmibh air an Tighearna airson cobhair' ('Call upon the Lord for help'), said one. 'Chan e am airson urnuigh e. Chan e sin a tha agad ri dheanamh ach tarruing air do ramh' ('What a time for prayer, that is not what you have to do, but to pull on your oar'), replied another. The *bodachs* ultimately got ashore.

Tormad Siosal was an old retired shepherd who lived in Glenhalten. The Halten was then a fruitful fishing stream and old Tormad knew every inch of the water. The small dorsal fin on the salmon is called '*deargadh*' and the fisher's remark, 'Cha d' fhuair mi deargadh' means, 'I got nothing.' Old Tormad (Norman) was known to account for many fish near his home. When he got a fish, he sliced off the dorsal fin and threw it into the river. When asked if he had got any fish during the season, he would declare, 'Cha d' thug mi dhachaidh deargadh am bliadhna.' ('I did not take a fin home this year.') He thus saved his somewhat elastic conscience.

At a *ceilidh* the talk was about the wiles and tricks of the fox. Many instances were told of Reynard's astuteness and enjoyed by young and old, each tale giving birth to further tales. One old *bodach*, Calum Breabadair, listened to each narrative and resolved not to be outdone by the younger members of the party, in adding zest to the *ceilidh*. Calum's welcome intervention was as follows:

The salmon fishers found that some of their fish were disappearing, and resolved to set a watch. On the first night, the lot fell on Iain Ban MacDhomhnuill. Iain repaired to the bothy and put up a roaring fire. He took off his boots, placing one on each side of the fire, lit his pipe and awaited developments. For a time, no sound broke the silence until, at length, a scraping sound reached Iain's ears from the far end of the bothy, and he was at once alert. Soon a fox appeared, carrying a grilse in its mouth. Iain sprang to block the hole at the foot of the door. The fox sprang forward, let go the fish, seized Iain's boot and dropped it into the fire. Iain sprang to rescue his boot. The fox picked up the grilse, was through the hole and off.'

Domhnull na Faochag (Donald of the Whelks) was a merchant but quite illiterate. When he sold an article on credit, he made a rough drawing of it in his 'day book'. A young man, going to the east coast fishing, got a jersey and a round cap from him. On his return, he called on Donald to pay him. Donald turned up his 'ledger' and said, 'A jersey and a griddle.' 'Griddle! What would I do with a griddle?' said the fisherman. 'I got a jersey and a cap.' 'Oh that's it,' said Donald, 'I forgot to add the ribbons to the ring.'

Two old men lived by themselves in Braes. They were not the type who earned for Skye its reputation for hospitality. One day they had a visitor, an old man whom they reluctantly invited in and proceeded to prepare the evening meal of thin porridge. This was served in three cogs or cumans, two of equal size and one smaller, which was handed to the guest. The guest finished and thanked his hosts. Handing over his cog he said, 'Na'm bitheadh an cuman sin blaidhna ann am Flodigaraidh, bhidheadh e uiread ri cach' ('If that cog was a year in Flodigarry, it would be as big as the others'), an allusion to the *bodachs'* meaness, and to the fertility of Flodigarry.

A wordly old man, who had never had a day's illness, fell suddenly ill. Fearing that his end had come, he sent for a neighbour, and requested him to read a chapter from the bible. The would-be comforter was as oblivious of his task as the sufferer, and read where the book opened, describing the destruction of the Philistines' corn. The old man was listening intently. At length he raised himself on his arm, and cried, 'Lies, John, big lies, where could they get that number of foxes!'

The following was related to me some years ago. A kindly old priest in one of the outer isles was one morning faced by his maidservant, saying someone had taken corn from the barn. 'Oh Mary, none of my people would do such a thing.' 'It has been done, however,' said Mary. A few mornings later, Mary made a similar announcement. Believing that Mary was probably right, the priest resolved to keep watch. Concealing himself in the corner of the barn, he awaited events. At length he heard footsteps, and the barn door was cautiously opened. The intruder bundled some corn in a rope, and quietly made his exit. The priest, stealing cautiously behind him, set fire to his burden, which soon blazed about his ears. In terror he threw it off, and hurriedly made for his home. By and by the man went to confession. He confessed delinquency after delinquency. When he ceased, the priest inquired if there were not others. 'No other,' said the man. 'Try and remember,' said the priest. At length, when persistently pressed, he said, 'I had not a bite for my cows, and I took a bundle of corn from your barn. As I was going off with it, the devil came up behind me and set fire to it!'

The Croft